Dissociative Fusion

Alyssa Nadolny

Act I

Dissociative Fusion

Poetry and Prophesy LLC
(Publisher)

First Edition May 2023
ISBN: 979-8-9882355-0-7

Illustrator: Sarah Baillargeon
sarahbaillart.com

Editor: Quincy "Q" Hull
stillblacksee@gmail.com
(901)212-6695

Designer: Ling Sigstedt
lingsigstedt.com

Alyssa Nadolny
PO Box 4071
Greenwood Village, CO 80155
www.poetryandprophesy.com

*Portions of this book are drawn from the author's memory.
Names, characters, places, and events have been changed to
protect personal privacy.*

A Note from the Author

This project has been 4.5 years in the making and has changed my life. Diagnosed with complex PTSD with structural dissociation in 2017, I worked relentlessly with therapists to desensitize and reprocess my past, present, and future using EMDR, neurofeedback and CBT therapy. This book started unknowingly in October 2018 after a nightmare I had of my father that made me start writing again after years of not being able to. (Nightmares and vivid dreams are very normal during EMDR processing). And then I just couldn't stop...the words kept pouring out.

This poetry book chronicles the initial voyage of my healing and dissection of various trauma. Over time, it began to resemble a clear story. I found my own fragmented memories and emotional parts in my poems beginning to resemble a coherent narrative. My true self and core slowly but surely beginning to emerge and bloom. I found my voice again and hope. I found forgiveness, grace, self-love, and inner peace. I found patience with the process because healing is never linear. Most importantly, I found myself.

If you read the first poem and then the last, you can see the stark differences in the voice. A girl versus a woman. Fear versus courage. Impotence versus power. Pulsating and undeniable growth. I hope whoever is reading this can find their own hope, inspiration, medicine, and perhaps, the courage to heal as you bear witness to the journey of my dissociative fusion. Thank you.

Thank You

Dear Younger Me,

Thank you for your grit. For your tears. For believing in yourself. For your vision when everyone else was blind to your greatness. I know how hard things got. It was lonely. It was scary. It was confusing. It was heart-breaking. But I want to tell you, as a living testament to your character in hard times: we slay the dragons. We make our wishes come true. We live a life we only ever dreamed of at one point. We heal. We transform. We grow. We stumble. We get back up again. But most importantly dear girl: We win.

We fucking win.

Thank you, for everything.

-Lys

Dedication

This book is for every woman that has been through trauma. For every girl that had her heart broken by her father, and the subsequent men she tried to use to fix the gaping hole he left in her. This is for every girl whose voice has been pushed down, ignored, and shamed. This is for the mothers that mustered the strength to leave. This is for the sisters that held you in their arms when you felt absolutely lost. This is for the girls that became women and vowed to break the cycle. This is for the girls that still believe in magic despite all the pain endured. For the ones who refuse to give up on love. The ones that refuse to give up on themselves. The ones who betrayed themselves. For those that struggle to forgive themselves. The ones that struggle to love themselves. The ones that do. The ones that refuse to give up on life. This is for every woman that has struggled to leave an abusive relationship. This is for every woman that has been lied to at 3 am. This is for the forgivers. This is for the MILSOs. This is for the girls that lost hope. This is for the girls in the throes of mental illness. This is for the girls who are lost. This is for the girls that have been sexually abused. Scared. Afraid. Unaware of their god given right to be powerful and beautiful. This is for the ones that refuse to keep their mouths shut. This is for the healers. This is for the givers. The takers. The bad asses. The savages. The nurturers. The survivors. The movers. The shakers. The doers. The mothers. The wives. The daughters. The granddaughters. The sisters.

This is for every woman.

Contents

i. Kiss of Destiny

Dissociative Fusion

You floated into my dreams last night
You resurrected from the dead
My mind still anxious, stomach in knots
With all the rationalizations you said

You bought back your house in Wolcott
Changing and rearranging the landscape
But you didn't touch a thing inside
A melody outside the realm of grit

You bought a trestle for your reefer leaf
I tried to remind you what happened last time
Your ears open but your mind closed off
Memories play off of a reel of grief

You gave me a lifetime of pain
Consumed by your substances
And chasing those empty dreams
My heart remembers and breaks again

Visuals cut, now I'm running down halls
Screaming your name, I catch a glimpse
Running past burnt children
Wired to a fence without wrawl

You're nowhere to be found

My knees collapse to the floor
Desperate. Bewildered.
I lose you again. Inconsolable tears
Doors lead to nevermore

My consciousness dissociates
From the month of your recidivate
But memories and somatization
Fuse in dreams and radiates

Those dreams become nightmares

And my heart runs in circles within
I scream these walls thin
I find you in men
Wolves in sheepskin

And I try to amend
In them
What I couldn't
Accrue from you

I annihilate all
Prospects of happiness

Because inside
My heart succumbs
To the story that
"I am unworthy"

You haunt my thoughts
And dreams
Move my body
Robotically

Fighting and Flighting
Because it's you who's
Piloting

I plead to God to
Find a way out

I want to heal
But my pain makes
Me heel
And stay right here

How do you forgive and forget?
When the first man you loved
Vices your heart cavity
Like a corset?

Overdosed on truth
I search for you

But I find no one
And it's just me
Alone.

Wrestling in my dreams
Running down halls
Screaming "Dad!"
At the top of my lungs

Cause a daughter just needs
Her father
When all is said and done.

Lessons

You taught me that men don't stay
Unless the stay is self-interested
I keep looking for flowers to bloom
But find beestings instead

Bystander

I wonder where the charade stops
And love begins
Jester, fool, you keep me smiling
But a mask unveils another mask

Why do you want me?
Yet... want others?
This house no longer a home
Wondering how forever lasts

Bystander in my own life
The crosswalk broken
I play roulette
And run across the road

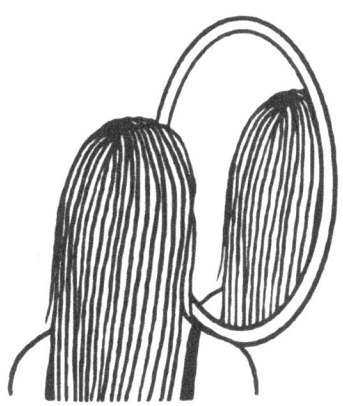

Liar.

Your voice feels like
My warm bath water
After 12 hours on my feet
I keep my eyes closed

Half child, half wolf
Your love innocent
Yet insatiable
I never get all of you

I bare my bones
And embrace your splinters
And rough edges
Even though they scrape me

I've never known
Such an honest liar

You can't love someone
That refuses to be loved
You can't hammer locks
That have never been picked

They say humans lie
The most during sex

You tell me you love
Me all the time

I only believe you
When I lock into your eyes
As I cum
And you whisper, "I love you."

Excruciating

My body is sore from uncovering my scars
Picking and scraping my exterior off
The sweetest pain I have never known

I have covered myself in layers
Upon layers
Hiding and protecting my soul

You saw right through me
You made my cold bones shake

I wanted to be alive again

Spectrum

I'm speaking in colors
To people completely colorblind

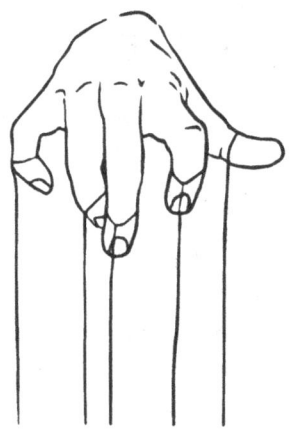

Rock Bottom

Here we find ourselves
At the bottom of the stairs
With gashes, black and blue
Wondering how we fell

Last thing I remember
Was the curtain of illusion
Lifting

And I saw the strings
Attached
The puppeteers were playing you

You let them.

Zombie

Walking among the dead
The sleeping
I find myself wondering
My mind stripping

The dead carry on
With their carry ons
And I wonder
Am I the one asleep?

Murderer

I bleed out & out
Until I run dry
Bloodless & cold
You wonder why I've changed

Cannibalism

You've managed to eat
My eyes
Yet offend when
I can no longer see
Your tries

Attention Deficit

Proverbious & perverted
I find that my mind
Tends to catch a
Case of the runs

Daydreaming out loud
My feet planted firmly
On the ground
But my head floats

Up, up & far away

Leaving my body behind
Concentration useless.

Abused Woman's Manifesto

I will not marry my father
I will not marry my father
I will not marry my father
I will not marry my father

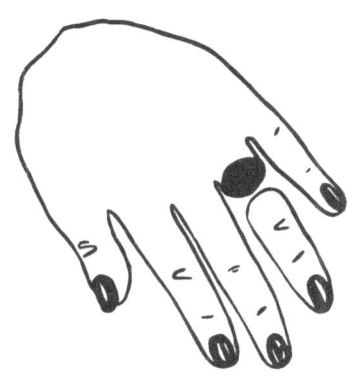

Cycle

Tell me mother, when did it hurt most?
When he came home at 3 am
Unfulfilled promises, empty
Or when God gave you daughters
And you watched him break their hearts too?

Goddess

I remember my mother crying as you left
Heartbroken yet she still spun magic
Enveloped us in her vast love
That you couldn't feel
Toddlers giggle and smile at her gaze
She never needed you. You needed her.
You can't destroy a goddess.

The Chariot

The wheel of fortune has its eyes on me
Owl perched, watching my next step
I step up into my destiny
The dancing elephants stomp their feet
The dried creek is rescued by water
The emperor tasks me with focus
My mother arms me with a sword
And a map to find my way back home
I'm coming home to myself

Direction

My father's foot on my mother's neck
Her father's foot on her mother's neck

Some would say it's in my blood
To bow down to a husband, my possessor

I have always had this inkling
That I was born into this sect

To conquer and defeat centuries of
Brokenness, to admonish the oppressor

Men above women
Women underneath men

I am whole on my own
A complete masterpiece

They fear what they can't understand
Or see

The beauty, voraciousness of love
Oozing, floating, dancing

I remind them of a wild animal

She stirred something in these men
Dormant since Adam and Eve

God sent to coax out their spirits
Relinquish control and ego power

They felt their masks slip, their souls awaken
Frightened yet intoxicated, they call her evil

Clipped wings, they tame her
Not to be trusted to roam free or rule

Centuries pass
Abuse persisted

So did her spirits
She has a job to do

No more bowing
Admonishing your wild, vast greatness

Unfold your wings young girl
Be the love you wish to see in this world

Self-Love

I thought I needed you to survive
My lifeline, oxygen
I never needed you
I needed myself

Runaway

You gave up on your love. Forsaken.
Too intense.
Too much accountability.
Too real.
You weren't ready for a woman.
So you ran.
But let me not mince words:
I am seared in the back of your mind
You will close your eyes and see my face
You will touch her skin and long for mine
She will distract you from your ache
But she will never make you feel your soul
That bitch will never be me.

Transgenerational Trauma

My Nana told me a story once
Of my great-great-grandmother
At age 14, a child bride
Who bore 17 children

She didn't drop a tear
When her husband died
They asked her what he was like
"He didn't believe in the word no."

Choices

Do you want to be a mom?
Do you want to be a mom to a husband?
Do you want to return to yourself?
Do you want to return to your heart and soul?

Birds of a Feather

What do you tell her
When she touches your tattoo
And asks what it means?

I tell everyone
Mine was an impulsive decision
On a trip to Miami

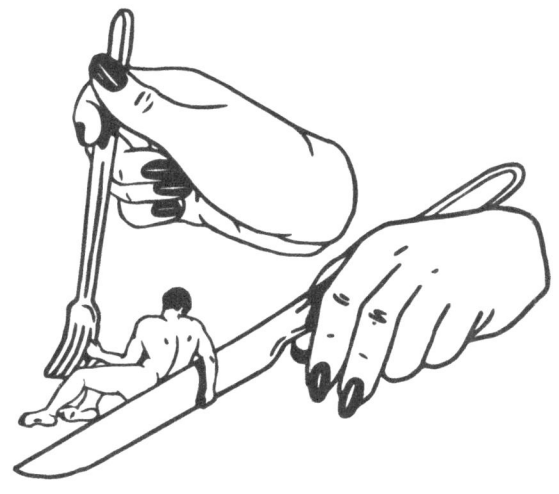

Maneater

Tired of men bitching
Of their ego bruise
Because I fucked them
Without feeling anything

Let's be honest, when we were naked
I saw the look on your face
You're only mad because
I decided there would be no third date

P.S. I don't want to feel anything

Dangerous

What do you call a female?
Who doesn't need anyone?

To the Women That Don't Like Me

I used to care what you thought about me
Until I realized my dog has more interesting
Things to say
And he can't even speak

Men That Self-Medicate

Help me to understand
How you came to decide
That numbing yourself
To play it safe
Was worth the trade off
Than being able to feel and
To be really fucking happy.

Freedom

My mom told me healing comes in layers
I've become obsessed with peeling the grief off
Every day without you hurts a little less
The unknown a little more exciting

I sit in stillness each morning
A cup of hot mint tea. A dab of raw honey.
The leaves rustle outside the open window
I don't feel lonely when I'm alone anymore

When He Comes Back

The problem is that I loved you more than I loved myself
The problem is that you wanted me all to yourself
The problem is that you needed me to love you so much
Because you don't know how to love yourself

You self-sabotage because deep down
You feel unworthy and undeserving.
What did they do to you sweet child?
What knots your stomach and makes you sweat?

I would stay and listen, help even
But the time it took you to come back
I had an unexpected growth spurt
Like an old jacket, you don't fit me anymore

#MeToo

I don't remember your face
Or your voice
But my body remembers
Subconsciously compartmentalized
My heart races as I try to retrieve a memory

Coercion is Rape

I hate the way you controlled me
Told me what to do
Dictated position after position
Fantasy confused for inhibition
I didn't know any better being young
You never asked for permission

I would fight you off
And you would plead and plead
Coerced me until I gave in
I felt dirty
Giving you head every night
You wanted to fuck me
Like we were in a porno

Raw.
Anal.
Cum on my chest.
Sadistically.

Pain.
Muscle constriction.
Holding my breath.
Obligation.

I was an object for you to violate.
Humiliate. Intimidate.

I believed I was your object
I rationalized and dissociated
I associated love with penetration
Blamed it on your lack of agnation

The best day of my life
Is when I told you to fuck off
After you told me it was my vocation
As your girlfriend to please you.
After I rejected you again.

Sex shouldn't hurt.

No.

Means no.

First Love

I'll never forget how small I felt
Curled in a ball
Half -naked on the floor
My face red, crying hysterically

As you towered above me
Screaming
Our weekly ritual at that point

I don't remember what you even said
But I do remember thinking to myself
"You're going to die if you stay here."
I almost lost my will to live

I decided in that moment
I was going to leave you

It took me two more years
And about 7 tries
But I finally left you
And I never looked back

When a Savior is Human

You saved me from him.
Showed me what respect looked like
Love felt like
Taught me sex is mutually beneficial
I clung to you like a life raft
But failed to see
You had short comings too

Second Love

I don't regret loving you
For a second
I regret nothing
I wish it worked out differently
But we both know
I have bigger stages to stand on
You have more healing to do
I forgive you. I hope you forgive yourself.
Thank you for all of the lessons
I will always love you.

Whatever and Wherever
the Fuck You Want

What do I do
Where do I go
Now that no man has any power over me?

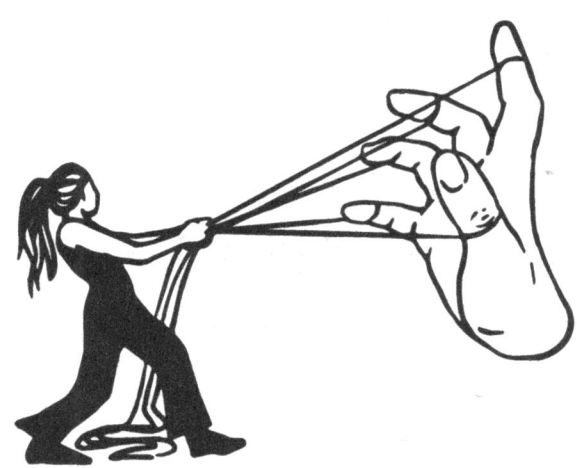

Forgiveness

Karmic ties from the past
Tend to hold your body back
Tend to keep your heart meek
But you're not mild

You're infectious and light
You are glorious and beautiful
You are forever the free
You are the capsule

Swallow that love whole
Laugh until it hurts
Your dark is just dimmed light
You are retribution in the flesh

You can right the wrongs of the past
You can heal and let go
You are all you need to be
All you have to do is forgive yourself.

How Secrets Lose Their Power

You can't hurt me anymore
But this black tar
Pits my stomach

You gave me needle and thread
And I pushed the needle into my lip
The thread follows through
The pierced hole

Your indiscretions through my soul

Bloody lips closed
I don't say a word

It's been six years
My doll smile fools
Everyone assumes I've self-soothed

The knotted thread pulls
And scabs crack
Every time I force a smile

I pretend the black tar
Isn't there
I pretend the stomach pain
Muscle spasms
Don't exist

It keeps hardening, boiling
Rotting my insides
Flesh meets the back of my throat

I woke up today
Decided I no longer
Wanted to bear the burdens
You imposed and promote

Each scissor snip brings relief
I open my emaciated mouth
Take a deep breath and scream
And I blackout

I remember waking up on the floor
Next to rusty scissors
Bloody, withered thread
My fingers reach past my tonsils

Until I cough, and gag
My fingers reach deeper into my esophagus
My stomach retching
And the tar comes projecting

Out

I watch the insides of my stomach
Lying on the floor
I wipe my mouth with my sleeve
And breathe a sigh of relief

Beware

I'm singing like a canary
About all the pain I carried

Slip Back Into a Dream

I never needed anyone
But today I ache in vain for you
I hate what you've done
But today I forsake pain for love

I see the corners of your smile
Turn up as I make you laugh
Memories haunt me daily
I just can't help it

You fell onto my lap
Out of nowhere
Divine timing
But soul contracts end

I scream in vain
For the memories
Yet to be made

I cry in pain
For our unborn child
I desperately craved

I wish we could turn back time
Know what we know now then
I'm wishing wishing for a sign
Know what I know about my friend

We cracked open our hearts
And the world caught on fire
Too impassioned and bridleless
We burned the damn thing into the ground

Quiet moments in your arms
Are all over now

Future of one
Because we broke in two
I wonder if you long for me
The way I still long for you

I know it's all over
The reality too abrasive
Slip back into a dream
Ignorance seductively persuasive

EMDR

I put the headphones on to go back
Binaural beats knock on the trap door
Of my implicit memories

I close my eyes
Take a deep breath in, exhale
The trap door swings open

My finger traces the line in the blue suede upholstery
My finger delves into the yellow cushion
Exposed from a burn

You tell me to not touch anything
You tell me to get back in the back seat

You're unusually nervous
On edge
You roll down the window

A man stands in the pitch black
"You brought your fucking kid?"
I sink and freeze into the passenger seat

I see Budweiser cans littered on the floor
Two bricks of cocaine
My curious two-year-old hands reach for them

You tell me not to touch anything
You tell me to get back in the back seat

Bender

My mother caught rain water
Leaking from the ceiling
With pots and pans
All alone

She paid bills
Raised two children
With her own two hands
All alone

Your Thursday paycheck
Would fly out the door
In your pocket
Turning up empty on Sunday

No one knew your ETA
Whereabouts elusively poor
But the job docket
Was punched in by Monday

Ego vs True Self

You wish upon a star
For a prince charming
On a white, noble horse
Searching their whole life

For you.

You eye each new man
With x-ray vision
If he's the one of course
Searching his whole life

For you.

You daydream
Place him on a pedestal
Call him the one
He'll make all your dreams come true

He'll fill that void
He'll kiss each cut
You couldn't look at
He'll make you feel whole

But each new season passes
Another turns out to be a mortal
By loneliness you're trapped
Again and again avoid your soul

They filled your head
With dreams of
Codependent
Aspirations

They tell you
As a whole child
You're inadequate
Cursed to lonely damnation

Without another's love

Everyone is looking for someone
The missing puzzle piece
The perfect partner
The perfect love

As though our flaws aren't beautiful
And make us masterpieces
The perfect partner
The perfect love

Is the relationship
You have with yourself

No one is coming to save you
No one can save you
No one will save you
Only you can save you

Learn who you are, what you are
Being alone doesn't equate loneliness
Learn to love yourself
Build yourself from the inside out

So no one can tear you down again
So you can break toxic familial cycles
So you can be healthy and happy
So you have a life you deserve

The real thing won't need you
And you won't need him
But you'll share yourselves
With each other anew

Watch how you love one another
Once you truly love you for you
There is no piece missing

Talking In My Sleep

Hierophant tell me what you see
Tetherless, standing in front of
Sleeping water
An eye casts its spell on me

Darkness envelops the air
The moon illuminates the umber
My bare feet step in
Disturbing its slumber

The depth swallows my body
I begin to fall up
I hold my breath
Holding out my cup

The current arouses
Licks down rocks
Floating on my back
Consciousness drowses

My father's sitting on the dock
His paw reaches for mine
Water lifts me out
And we begin our sleepwalk

Father of wands revealed
We dance our wounds exposed
Listen to the bubbling brook's song
He medicines my bones healed

The sun's rays begin to stretch
Locking eyes, his head nods
Look for the synchronicities
Your dreams are the catch

To My Unborn Child

Someday when you're old enough
You'll see crow feet around my eyes
From every belly laugh
Every empty, desolate cry

Your finger will trace my scars
As you lie in my arms
Someday when you're old enough
You'll understand

When you're old enough I'll tell you
How you picked me off of the floor
Half dead, giving me strength
To walk out of my abuser's door

When you're old enough I'll tell you
How I broke my own heart
And locked the door on my soulmate
Because he wasn't good enough for you

Someday I'll tell you about my solitude
How I learned to love myself
Drained my own blood
Picked my rotting flesh

You'll learn how I danced with my demons
Stopped running from the devil's hooves
And stared him down
Took my power back

Someday you'll see, you have always been
The love of my life
My infinite inspiration
Everything I did was for you

Remembrance.

The hour glass sand slides and collects
My tears don't come anymore
Remembering all you've done for me
Disgust collects in my throat, burning

Screams ricochet off of plexiglass
Your insatiable appetite for destruction
Has indefinitely become your legacy
I burn your playbook, learning

Anger sears my chest from the outside in
I no longer pity you
You reaped what you sowed
And left us here with merely nothing

I no longer care to understand your demons
I've tried to befriend them once before
They sat on my chest while I slept
And I drowned in your sorrow and emptiness

I wish I could say I'm surprised
But your absence was the only consistency
You provided to your own children
You painted ugliness but sold them as Picasso

I wish I could claim I'm at peace
But I ate the food from the palm
That fed me, infected me
I could almost be as sick as you

Borderline M.

Broken men, broken promises
I hate to love you
I hate to need you
I ache for freedom
I ache for love
I ache for bones
I hate your love
I hate your bones
I feel nothing
I feel everything
Generations of broken men
Silenced mothers
I feel the weight heavy
To be different
To break chains
I cannot rest
Or lie down
Generations of trauma
Abuse
Neglect
Silence.
I'm screaming your names now
And I can't stop

Florence.

Ma, you can breathe now
It wasn't in vain
I won't allow
Another broken beast
To rob the crown

Everything Is Love

I closed my eyes and breathed gently
I took each impaled weapon
Out of my own flesh
And I started anew

I cleansed my soul
Letting go of the grief
Letting go of the anger
I am complete, I am whole

I don't need you to say anything
Learning to forgive you.
I love you
And I release you

God intertwines paths for lessons
Pain is the greatest teacher
A catalyst for change
Change is his blessing

I used to sit defeated
Scorn the sky and scream so broken
Victim mentality stuck
I now see that I am chosen

Forged from the fire
You made me an example
That no matter what hell we walk through
The human spirit is indestructible

No matter what tomorrow brings
Sorrow, joy, pain, bliss
Everything is a gift
Everything is a lesson

Everything is love.
I am so grateful.
I am so grateful.
I am so grateful.

To My Future Husband

I have yet to see your face
But I already love you
I have yet to hear your story
But I already know your heart

I can't wait to finally meet you

It's Time

I need to thank each one of you
That showed me darkness
Rejection
Fear
Loneliness
Isolation
Self-destruction
Your chaos and indiscretions
Revealed under layers upon layers

The movie plays again without any skips
I'm finally the director
In my own life
Fortitude
Grace
Gratitude
Self-acceptance
My power no longer for sale
My inner peace no longer up for a debate

I wear my skin lovingly, I am completely free
Comfortable in my own shoes
Revealed to myself
I am infinite
I am not my body
I cry tears of relief realizing
I am finally found, I am finally home to myself

Ego

You thought your healing was done?
Complete?
Silly fool, I am a magician
Elusive, deadly

You barely scraped the surface
Of the horrors in your head
After denial comes
Reality to slap you awake

Coffee

Three hours of talking
Alleged healing
Dissecting our failures
Could have, should have

We pull together like magnets
Completely illogical
Utter passion
Chaos and riots ensue inside

I feel dizzy
Don't look at me that way
Don't inch any closer
Because I still love you

F5

I dream of tornados now
Destructive cyclones
Whipping out of thin air

I watch from the window
Bracing for impact
The backroom catching fire

I run to the backroom
Grabbing the only thing I care about
Choking on inhaled smoke

Running down the stairs
Safely out the door
I never look back

Phoenix

No one hears my cries this morning
Alone in my bed
The rain outside patters
Soothing and drowning the chest heaving

A night with you
Ignites years of raw, suppressed emotions
Rejection, humiliation, disrespect
Boils my stomach

You sing songs of remorse
Unable to comprehend my wounds
You've imposed and allowed
Yet you want to come home

You lay claim to misery without me
But when you had me in your arms
I felt you slip a million miles away
You want your cake and to eat it too

You can't look me in the eye
Or touch the scar on my back
From the knife you placed there
Four and a half years ago

Your love a mental prison
You led me in with bread crumbs
Of hopes, dreams, and taboo desires
Locked away as your pretty bird

But I like the Quetzal
Die in captivity
I don't belong to you
I belong to the ether

You thought I was a baby elephant
That you could tether and train
To be more like your own kind
Yet I became the circus freak

And so, I set myself on fire
Self-imposed self-destruction
Burning the cage down with me
And from ashes I rise

Never to return

Drowning

Pipedreams you had no intention of
Promises you never intended to keep
Love you never wanted to work for
Depth you couldn't swim to

Latin Tattoos

We had the world at our fingertips
That time we first clicked
A smoky July night
Do you remember the boy you were then?

Change

I ask myself why I held on for so long
When you tried swinging me off your back
Dr. Jekyll Mr. Hyde complex
I fought to crack you wide open

You need me the way
My father needed my mother

Loyal to a fault
I held it down
While mortars imploded
All around you

I became your only sense of normalcy
While you danced with destruction
And howled the chaos in
Taking me down with you

I thought the worst was over
The moment you returned home
How foolish and naïve of me
The war was just the beginning

Homecoming

You slept straight on your back
Heard phantom explosions
As you tried to fall asleep
You promised you were fine

Are you the same boy
I said goodbye to
Professed my love to
Ten months before?

Your eyes don't glimmer
Your smile forced
Smoking Marlboro Reds
As if your life depended on it

I laid my head on your chest
Eyes closed, listening to your heart beat
I inspected your silhouette as you slept
Many nights, grateful you were safe

I was unaware to the fact
That you died in that desert
The man sleeping next to me
Was an imposter of your ghost

Veteran

How do you mourn the dead
With air still in their lungs

Repeat Offender

I want to forgive
In the worst way
But I just
Can't forget

Rebound.

How does it feel realizing
That for five months
He was imagining me
Every time he penetrated you?

I tried to warn you
Your burns would be inevitable
I tried to tell you
He would not love you

But you thought you were special
Didn't you?
What you had was different
Didn't you?

Such a naïve fool
You had yet to scrape the surface
Of the chameleon that lied next to you
I warned you so.

How does it feel realizing
I know him better
Than he knows himself?
I told you so.

Heroin

Tourniqueted dreams like your arms
Punctured hope like your skin

What would I become
Without my hero?

Your accidental overdose
My purposeful strength

Your kryptonite revealed
I am my own heroin(e)

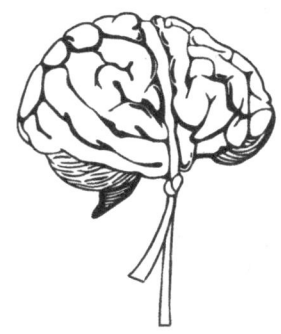

Amnesia

I debride you from my chest
A wound festering my heart
I let myself bleed out
In the hopes I die
And wake up
In a dimension
Where I don't know your name
Or recognize your face

"Wow, you're so strong."

Who was your father?
An elusive man short on promises

What did he expect you to be?
Strong. Sharp. Resilient. Honest.

Who did he expect you to be?
The person he could never be.

Who are you?
I don't know anymore.

The Root of Rage

You burn a thousand homes
With a flick of your tongue

Kill it before it kills you
Weak, egotistical mentality

You despise the rat race
Yet daily tighten your laces

Exalting abuse and selfishness
Yet you crawl in your own skin

An entitled selfish brat
Her words became your inner dialogue

Disconnected and unsatisfied
Inadequate and empty

You have failed yourself
You have failed yourself

Wake up.
Get up.

Kill it before it kills you
She's killing you

The Masochist

How many more men will you use up?
Try to change them into self-medication?
Knowing full well they are limited?
You're addicted to the pain, aren't you?

Who's to Blame?

I am
I am
I am
I am

Pointing in the Mirror

You're a cocky motherfucker
For someone so insecure

Accountability

I've allowed the trauma
To change
My honey lips
To turpentine

I've allowed this beating heart
To turn off
Blacken
Harden

I've allowed love
Friendships
Connectedness
To slip through my fingers

I scream the name of men
I label my jailors
Demanding to be released
From my prison

Funny though

I'm the one
Starving myself out of fear
I'm the one
Holding my keys to freedom

Inner Dialogue

Are you ready to merge?
To truly heal?
Are you ready to let go?
To forgive yourself?

Spirituality

Truth be told
Love is the answer

Transcend your ego
Change your perspective

Quiet your mind
Change your thoughts

You are loved
You are love

Inner Child

Sweet girl,
Where did you go?
Where are you hiding?
I promise it's safe to come out

Death Grip

Holding onto the pain in a death grip
Locked away in your subconscious
Always on high alert for risk
But you force a smile through caution

What would happen if you just relinquished?
Why are you afraid to put down your knives?
Your demons will stay extinguished
As long as you illuminate your life

Let go, the fabricated need to control
You are not threatened
Let go, the logical need to outwit
Lay down your weapons

How tired are your bones
Doing it your way?
How lonely are your days
Locking yourself in a cage?

Let go.
Breathe. Surrender.
Let go.
Be. And render.

Misogyny

How dare I speak what's on my mind
How dare I illuminate my light
How dare I raise my voice
How dare I stand in my truth

Intimidating or intimidated?
Bitch or Alpha?
Good ole boy or Beta?
Tip toe on eggshells or timid?

Hell yeah 'I don't need a man'
But I get one when I want one
Perhaps that's where your disdain lies
Knowing I would never choose you

Innately, I hold the power
And given the chance
You'd be eating out of the palm of my hand
Wouldn't you?

Processing

With all of the hurt inside your heart
All of your discernment that led you astray
What did you learn?

Through all of the tears you have shed
Every connection that fate severed
What did you learn?

With all the regret you carry
All of the shame and guilt worn
What did you learn?

Through all of the storms you endured
Wiping out all you had ever known
What did you learn?

With all the red flags you ignored
All the hope that rendered you foolish
What did you learn?

Through all the strength you had to muster
Picking yourself up by your own boot straps
What did you learn?

With all the love you experienced
All the love you lost
What did you learn?

Through all of the violated boundaries
The subsequent scars you inherited
What did you learn?

With all of the lies you believed
All the manipulation you fell prey to
What did you learn?

Through all of the darkness you have walked
Learning to irradiate light from within
What did you learn?

Caught in the Ruins

Emotionally violent lovers
Separate to take a break
From lobbing each other's hearts
Through poignant windshields

The dust begins to settle
Here we are sitting in our corners
Bloody, battered, and bruised
Still unwilling to throw in the towel

Confined inside a caged octagon
Pride keeping the chords connected
Our souls dying from destruction
Yet we still call it love

The dust begins to settle
My ears ringing, and I can't see
Resentment sits on my back
I just wanted him to let me in

I thought my torturer would be my tonic
I thought it was true love's tune
But instead he shows me a mirror
And I show him his own

The dust begins to settle
Soulmates clout each other awake
The only way out is in
I refuse to die here and call it a life

Alone.

Somedays the tears don't make sense
And I wonder if I only have myself to blame

Letting Go

Holding apart the trap's jaw
Sweating, crying
Bleeding fingers press against its teeth
An ankle finally free
Run

Don't put your ankle
Back in a trap once it's free
Don't put your heart
Back in his hands once it's free
Run

Transparency

Deception is your tool
Magic chameleon
You play your game well
Lost soul

Parasite to warmth
Moth to light
Trapped by ego
I see right through you

Wishing Well

I wish I knew how to show my softness
Without clawing others

I wish I knew how to speak my truth
Without using a sharp tongue

I wish I knew how to love
Without being someone's fool

I wish I knew how to be myself
Without watering it down

I wish I knew how to think clearly
Without being impulsive

I wish I knew how to trust others
Without resorting to pulling away

I wish I knew how to heal
Without blaming someone else for these wounds.

Sunshine

I don't drop tears for you anymore
My stomach doesn't churn in acidity
My emotions leveled
You can't dance them dizzy

My heart doesn't yearn for you anymore
My mind doesn't race itself
My mind leveled
You can't keep me busy

Love is everywhere I look
You can't offer what I don't already have
The wind has blown the chaos away
And inner peace is ushering in

Strength is everywhere I look
You don't amount to what I already am
The clouds have parted halfway
Allowing the sun to shine within

Healing.

How many more layers can I peel off of
myself until there's nothing left?

Nobility

There's immense strength
In knowing
What you're made of

Yellow Bird

Clear your throat
Take a deep inhale
Speak loudly & clearly
Your voice is a gift

Woke

Last Wednesday I wished for an ego death
Exhausted from fear's law
Last Wednesday I took a final breath
Maggots in my mind begin to gnaw

Thursday morning I opened my eyes
Feeling astral planning fatigue
Thursday morning I was still alive
Then carried on without intrigue

By Saturday I was living in love
Laughing, consumed by light
By Saturday I released all fears above
Focused forward, my future bright

On Monday I shared curative hands
My power growing in strength
On Monday a Voodoo queen showed me lands
I had long forgotten at length

By Wednesday I took a walk down memory lane
Storylines playing without a break
By Wednesday I released ancient pains
I am irrevocably entirely awake

Meditation

Giving permission to walk away
Giving permission to stand tall
Giving permission to forgive all
Giving permission to openly pray

Sweet Peas

Eyes shut, pink flowers blossom
I smell your perfume Great Grandma
Standing on top of a mountain
Showing me, I'll conquer them all

Ivory walls carved with symbols
Extend each way past my sight
Dreams of amulets
Telling me I'm not alone

Root Chakra

Thumbs drag down the side of my thigh
Decades of harbored emotions
Come flooding out
I hold my breath and wince

Painful release but I can let go
Purple lilacs fill new spaces
Uprooting stagnant energy
I can begin to plant my garden

Grounding myself
Healing the body
Freeing dense sentiments
I put a name to a feeling

Top soil turning
My hips loosen and open
Connecting mind to body
I trust the process

A Moment

The veil of fog thinning everyday
Stepping into my power more and more
Realizing and remembering who I am

Dark skies illuminate the crescent moon
I'm holding my chest
Admiring the glowing beauty

Pink light washes my body
Welcoming its vitality
I smile for myself now

Entitled & Toxic

Knocking on the door
Like you still own the place
Lingering at the entrance
Like I would still let you stay

Denial runs deep in your mind
I don't have the patience
Certainly not the time
Wondering about your intentions

He asked me if I still feel butterflies
When I see your face
When I see your face
All I feel is your betrayal

Still learning to love you
Like Jesus loved Judas
Still learning to forgive
Someone so venomous

Dry

Loneliness grips my chest
The song plays a moment in my mind
Heavy on the heart
The drinks have hit me

I don't want to find you in any corner
Of me, my mind, my soul
I'll never drink again
So long as I'll never have to think of you again

Manipulation

I caught a spider in my dream
Admired the graveyard in his web
Failing to notice this decoy
Prey to your flow and ebb

"You'll Find Someone Better"

Since we broke up
Some people tell me how much
They always thought
You were a douchebag

Truth Hurts

A lot of men don't want to love women
They just want to have the upper hand

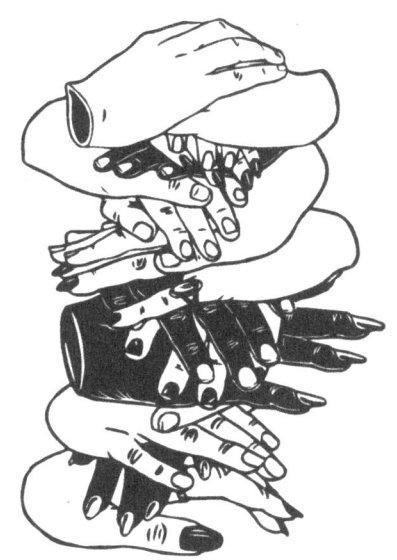

Waiting

Tell me you're really real
That you really do exist
Balanced sex appeal
Not intimidated by closed fists

Tell me you know how it feels
Therefore, you would never hurt me
Always honest and keeping it real
Understanding my need to be free

Loving me for all that I am
And all that I'm not
Gentle as a lamb hands
Everything on the line, all that you've got

A woman with a wild heart
Needs a man with a wild soul
You would never let me fall apart
I would never let you grow cold

Please tell me you're still out there
Waiting for the day we finally meet
I'll never give up, I wouldn't dare
Hoping you exist somewhere, man of my dreams

Boundaries

The abused often become abusers
I have your smile and your frown
I understand why, I truly do
But I am holding my ground

You're not responsible
For how the trauma made you feel
But you are responsible
For choosing how you heal

I need you to dry your face
And start digging deep
I'm not your keeper or savior
But your wounds have started to seep

I am responsible for my well-being
And you are for yours
I'm simply asking for a knock
Instead of busting through the door

Enmeshment and codependent habits
I'm cutting toxic chords
Familial cloths and generational fabric
I'm stronger than I've ever been before

Unafraid to walk alone in my truth
Cutting teeth on a diamond in the rough
This defined insanity, if you only knew
Refusing to participate, enough is enough

Star Glow

I wanna grab your face with my hands
Tell you stories all night
My face in your neck during a slow dance
Both feeling more than alright

Tell me boy, what do you see
When you look at the dark sky
I just want you all over me
Star glow dim compared to your light

I miss being in love.

But I'm happy hanging by myself

Restored Self-Esteem

I laugh and cry
Simultaneously

When I realized
My dad was right

When he said
No one was good enough for me

Coal Pressure

Silhouettes windmill
Merry-go-round
Facades revealed
Scary go down

Cigarettes and Advil
For a moment
At odds, hearts sealed
Tree trunk omen

Porch rain patter
Calming nerves
Colored dreams shattered
None of it deserved

Pain drops scattered
Healing reserved
Blurred lines battered
Strength preserved

Apathy

Treasoned promises lost
Reasoned excuses bought
Hands thrown up
Trance to letup

Can't plan for the weather
Plant roots to band together
Rusty hacksaw to chords
Blood drip in floorboards

Relief when sleeping
Inner thought creeping
Embracing universal love and magic
Retracing steps through traffic

Second chances and doors locked
Reckoned truth and chaos stopped
Unconditional love lost
Recreational act cost

Blossom

Sleepwalking all night
Telling you all the things
I can't say when we're awake
Hugging you one last time

Dreams that confuse and fright
Saying farewells to kings
Letting guards down to feel the ache
All of my tears have dried

Stuck in a space where
The past has ended
But the future has yet to begin
Sitting with the unknown and discomfort

Putting my hands in a prayer
You're easily offended
But I stick up my chin
A small justice for all I've suffered

Rather Be

Dancing in summer rain
Eyes closed, my face feels wet
Smile wide, I can't complain
Heart open, all in on one bet

No clue of what's to come
Making peace of the past
Accepting what wasn't succumbed
Abundance coming up fast

A Daughter's Love

I know if you were still here
You would tell me you're sorry
You would make me Nutella toast
In the kitchen having a party

I know if you were still here
You would still hold my hand
We would catch up for hours
Hang out with Uncle Jon and Dan

I know if you were still here
You would be in love with your grandsons
Admire how amazing of a mother Ash is
Teaching us all how to have fun

I know if you were still here
You would have dried my tears
Attempted to avenge my heartbreak
Settling for a heart to heart over beers

I know if you were still here
You'd push my shoulders back
Forcing me to stand up tall
Talk me off the ledge, keep me on track

I know if you were still here
You'd brag and say how proud I make you
You'd be the fuel to my fire
Cheering me on for every dream I pursue

I know if you were still here
You would tell me to forgive everyone
You'd tell me life's too short
To stay angry and hate everyone

I know if you were still here
I would soak in every moment
Take mental pictures of your smile
We would fix everything that was broken

I wish you were still here
I know you hear me when I pray
Always holding you close in my heart
I miss you more than words can say.

We're All Just Trying to Desperately Cope

Monsters are usually just women and men
Severely wounded children underneath
No longer intimidated by sharp teeth
I see your golden light time and again

Patience

Heart holding and healing
Takes time to take
On the way to the other side
Trusting universal methods

The beginning of my feeling
Was hard to shake
Now I'm along for the ride
Fear thrown in the air suspended

Taking root within myself
Growing out my hair and self-love
Looking healthy and feeling beautiful
Dancing off an old me

Wanna swim the continental shelf
Of my confidence they tried to get rid of
Happiness constantly presumable
Life like a sunset by the sea

Manifesting

I'm going to receive every single
Thing I have ever dared to dream
Watch me.

ii. Crossing the First Threshold

Wishing You Well

I hope you find the ocean fronts
And land the life you're looking for
I hope your feelings don't shunt
When you have a good woman you adore

I hope you learn to lasso dreams
Instead of places you can't see
I hope you say what you mean
(And not what everyone wants you to be)

I hope you learn to swallow your pride
And live up to your potential
I hope you look back and smile
Knowing lessons can be influential

I hope you can let me go with grace
Learning to move on with your life
I hope in this world you find your place
Learning how to spread your wings and fly

Premonition

I feel new energy pulsating
Something big is coming up
I have this funny feeling
My world is about to change

Power

Hearing music for the first time
After they said the music died
Bringing tears to my eyes
A symphony pulsing inside

A drum kicking in my chest
Songs waking up from rest
Hitting notes effortlessly
It's always been within me

Heart

Sharing your love
With the world
Ready to heal its hurt
Cause you're whole, baby girl

Pinot Noir

I'm slowly learning
I'll never be able to
Cut you out of my cloth
I'll wear this Pinot stain forever

1000 years older than Cabernet
Related to Chardonnay
I find you in everyone I drink
Tannins add a longer runway of life

When they ask where it hurt the most
I'll point to your spill
A timeless classic
My favorite bittersweet burn

Betting on Myself

A man once told me this anecdote:
    They don't bring the thoroughbred
    Right into the Kentucky Derby
    They run it through the mud
    A little bit first

Speaking My Truth

If time has taught me anything
It is imperative
You don't ignore red flags
When they wave in your face

When Abusive Men Attempt
to Make You Prey

Obsessive and jealous
One date in and you say
You've never met anyone
Quite like me

The flattery a distraction
From the fact that
You're trying to
Lay me into a trap

You don't even know who I am
On paper, I look like every man's dream
But men like you get a nightmare
They never saw coming

This isn't my first go around
And since you underestimated me
I'm going to play with my food
Before I chew and spit you out.

One Foot in Front of the Other

I'm free and riding the waves
Coasting alone and content
My chest still sore
But I'm still breathing

Sitting in on an adventure
I look around and see smiling faces
Time standing still for a moment
And I wonder where you are today

Mutual Friends

I tell Billy old stories of us
He laughs because he gets it
But I wonder if I'm telling our tales
Cause I'm afraid they'll die if I don't

Irony

Tears of joy and agony release
When I realize I had to lose you
In order to love myself
Soul feeling split in two

In the Throes of Grief

The anger is gone.
I've stopped searching in vain
For a way out of this
Reality of the inevitable
Has begun to finally set in.

James Hudson

We built such
Beautiful dreams
Didn't we?

I grieve each one
That we couldn't birth
Into fruition

They were right at the tips
Of our fingers
Slashed away

I hope all of your
Dreams come true
Someday

Muscle Memory

I'm trying to invest in a new reality
But you keep coming to me in dreams

No Contact

I wonder if the regret eats you alive
I wonder if you wish for a do over
I wonder how your pride abuses you
I wonder if I imagined the whole thing

Taction

I keep trying to find a man
That helps me forget you

But his arms don't compare to yours
His eyes aren't my favorite color

His hand doesn't fit in mine
As effortlessly as yours

His voice doesn't feel like home
His laugh doesn't fill me

His kiss makes me crave yours
His touch alien and lackluster

He wants to love me and treat me right
But I can't stop thinking about you

You're all I know how to love
My nose burns as the tears form

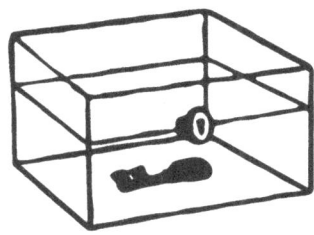

Overcoming Codependency

Pain exorcised from my body
Praying on my knees
Atonement for past sins
Ritualistic swearing to the entity

Commanding its departure
Unwilling manipulation
Possesses me to harm myself
Deeply entrenched

Secret knowledge of tongues
It begets me and eats me alive
But the negativity is driven out
Ancient practices heal and protect

Mitigate

Rubbing each bead
Between thumb and index
Chanting mantras
Cross legged

Connecting deeper within
Outside noises stop
Inner voice booming
Lighting the way

Growing

Driving under a hazy sun
Passing choppy waters
Three hawks hover above
Snow blankets the earth

Nails dig into the steering wheel
Glancing at moss bearding trees
Happy and contented moments
Funny how much changes in a year

Blurring the Lines

Temptation with potential
To come into fruition
Feeling out of control
Without any remorse

Kindred Spirits

Our laughter feels like
Childhood memories

Waves

My longing ceased to exist
Sorrow took the back exit
But one old song is all it takes
To have feral memoirs flood back

Fingertip Pulse

Black energy pointed upwards
From the ceiling to the floor
Purple flowers dissipate aroma
Creaks in floorboards sharp

Picturesque day painted
Hallowed trunks with gaping holes
Dark night images play
Forward movement stalled

Selfish eyes behold gluttony
Hellish death for lovers
She held you in, together
Loose string now knots your noose

Moon Eyes

Strength of one thousand suns
Coursing through the essence
Running late, arriving on time
Look how far you've come

Haunted House

I started sleeping on your side of the bed
So I could try to hold onto you every night

I see your ghost in the kitchen smiling
I can still hear your laughter and singing

I can still see you reading on the couch
With your morning coffee and bed head

I moved the furniture around in the loft
So I could stop seeing you upstairs

You still sit on the porch in the mornings
So I keep the blinds closed until noon

Cuban coffee tastes like Miami mornings
Holding hands, so I stopped sipping it

The dog lays his head on my chest
And I see his head on yours

Your mailbox key hangs from the hook
As if you still check it every other day

The front door still slams as loudly as the day
You walked out of it as your home for the last time

The shower still muffles my cries and chest heaving
So the neighbors can't hear a heart's sorrow

I burned the last photograph of you
But I close my eyes and dream of you

Where I smell you. Hold you. Love you.

Firefly

You are too powerful and bright
To be stuck in someone's jar

Father.

Every time I miss him
I wonder if it's you
I'm secretly mourning

Don't Marry Your Father

Unless you're into
That cyclic abuse
Type of thing

-marry yourself

Daylight Savings

Betrayal feels a lot
Like stolen time

Dust Storm

Furious sand pelting
Whittles a canyon
Exquisiteness emerges
From pandemonium

Crystal Visions

Underwater world spying from blue depths
I press my ear to your outside world
My ballgown waving as I gently tread
Watching you dance from a distance

Sisterhood

The women in my life
Cast magic and love
In a world full of darkness
A world full of fear

The women in my life
Have impenetrable spirit
In a world determined
To break them

The women in my life
Hold homes on their bare backs
Strength of a thousand lions
Softness of a thousand flowers

The women in my life
Have unbridled passion
Devastating scorn
The grace of royalty

The women in my life
Are messy and real
Lovely and cracked
Vibrant and magnificent

A.

Few opinions I take to heart
So when she finally advised me
To not take you back again
I listened.

Emotional Intelligence

The words you choose
To speak matter
Just as much as
Words unspoken

The Sadist

How many more women will you use up?
Try to make them into self-medication?
Knowing full well you're limited?
You're addicted to the chaos, aren't you?

Not Your Momma

Over needy men that try to guilt me
Over broken men that want to be fixed
Tie your own sutures darling
It's not my duty to restore you

Did I Stutter

I'll say it once
And I'll say it again:
            I will never need you.

-Louder for the men in the back

Unbothered

I bathe myself in love
Soaking in the kindness
Already have all I need
You want to impress me?

-Then inspire me

Shoaling

You move like a school of fish
Saying there's safety in numbers
Group-think mindless, easy
But you lose your identity

Monday Morning Podcast

Dreams are easy and free
But motion causes friction
Don't let small people
Pull you into constriction

Sacred Root

Turmeric pigments everything it touches
Indisputable gold consuming all surfaces
Is that how my forfeited love haunts you?
Indisputable gold consuming all parts of you

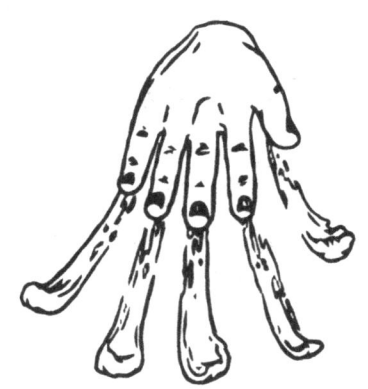

Queen Bee Copulating

I guarantee you've never
Had a woman like me
If you had, you wouldn't
Have lived to tell the tale

Vain Distractions

How much does it tear you up inside
Each time you bed a new flower
Stoned on the freedom you sought
Satisfied in immediate gratification

But in the morning, the high collapses
Your head and heart start throbbing
And all you can think about
Is how much you miss me

Unapologetic Standards

He accuses me of hating men
Claims my perception is jaded
Privileged, he hasn't been
Overpowered and overlooked

Privileged, he hasn't
Had hopes and dreams crushed
He hasn't been let down for decades
He hasn't been forgotten about

Privileged, he hasn't
Been lied to at 3 am
He hasn't been stuck in
Generational cycles of abuse

I'm not shrinking myself ever again
To make another man feel taller
I am a whole lot of woman
And I won't apologize for that

I love men, I believe in men
And their ability to heal, overcome
I just refuse to accept
Their bullshit behavior anymore

Survivor

You don't get to judge
How we came out the other side
You didn't see all the things
We had to do, the sacrifices made

In order to get by
Hiding papers in mattresses
Hiding the shame and embarrassment
Crossing t's, dotting i's

The white lies we told
Just so we could endure
Just so we could get out
Tip toeing through the door

Away from familiarity
Away from our living hells
Into the night, into the unknown
While our abusers sleep soundly

Fall Down 7 Times, Stand Up 8

The statistics say
A woman will attempt
To leave her abuser
At least seven times
Before she is finally free

Are you keeping count?

29 Miles to Go

Pull over
Reroute
Reconfigure
Proceed

Birthday Wishes

I was a success story
The day I decided
I was going to be happy
No matter what

I was not a success story
The day you decided
I made enough progress
To deserve your recognition

Conquering Myself

Victory is not linear
It's blood
Sweat and tears
Dragged through the mud

It's being destabilized
So shaky foundations
Can reconstruct
Into solid ones

It's failing
Over and over
But refusing
To lie down

It's messy and chaotic
But beautiful and poetic
It's jagged and coarse
But sweetly undeniable

Law of Attraction

Did you forget what I said
When you broke my heart?

>   Enjoy my tears while they last
>   Because someday they will dry and stop

>   One day you won't have a hold on me
>   Cause I'm a motherfucking juggernaut

That was a promise, not a threat
Can't stop tables from turning

Molting

I used to think picking my layers off
Was exhausting and made me raw
Feeling naked, vulnerable
Without stratums of pain

I've come to realize in time
I was simply shedding skin
That was never mine to wear
In the first place

My Therapist

Told me it was okay
To have fun, live my life
To do some slutty things

And honestly, that's
The exact type of support
I need in my life right now

The Butterfly

Stepping out of my chrysalis
My joints ache from the slumber
But my god it feels amazing
When I stretch open my wings

I'm Really Okay

I'll never forget
What happened to me
But what happened to me
No longer consumes me

I no longer sit around
And piss vinegar
Keep everyone out
Screaming 'Why me?'

My story is full of experiences
My god how much I'm learning
Beginning to feel at peace
With my past

Vigor

My memories no longer fragmented
My responses no longer reactions
Learning to live in each moment
Learning to make myself happy

Possibilities

Blank pages fill my novels
Unwritten memories and
Unspoken whispers
Just waiting for ink to touch

Fearless

I was put through hell
And then some more
To show the devil
I'm nothing to fuck with

Reestablished

It used to be difficult for me to make eye contact
I squandered my voice, afraid to ruffle feathers
Today, I stand taller with my shoulders back
And my loud voice projects and booms

Hooch and a White Horse

I'm not mad at you for being you anymore
The world had made its mind up
You tried as hard as you could I suppose
But your broken heart needed a crutch

Your brown sugar burnt
More than caramelized spoons
Had mama living in color, living in red
She couldn't find a better man

But mama never lied about loving you
She would've lassoed the moon
To illuminate your light if she could
Always prayed you'd pull through

But you were mad and stoned
Pushing her beyond her limits
She wanted to smack you awake
But you wanted to smack your veins

Backed into a corner she didn't want
You left her no other choice
With two babies to raise
Than to pack her bags and leave

All those years later, your pretty girl
Still cried hysterically for you and all of
The dreams that would never come true
The day the dragon smoked you out from the world

Peter Pan

I could never hate you
More than you hate yourself
At war with your reflection
Since the day you died inside

Floating through life
By the skin on your back
Latching onto any type of light
That will take a stranger in

Lost boy in the deep woods
Avoiding the lost and found
Avoiding being saved by grace
You never want to grow up

You only feel alive
With dirt in your eyes
Sugar in your blood
Flying back to mystical lands

Boastful and careless
Childhood selfishness
Stuck on repeat
You never quite get it

Watching you wrestle
In your dream state
Life a living nightmare
You know no peace

Nash Street Damage

I could never quite get
Relationships right
Until I accepted the fact
That you were a pathological liar

I could never quite get
Over the fact that
You relapsed in front of us
Until you died in front of us

I could never quite feel
Empathy for you
Until I realized that you
Were probably dissociating

I could never quite
Forgive you until
I allowed myself to
Hate you for a little bit

Insecure

I think you lied to your daughters
So you could pretend to be the man
You wanted to be inside your head
But you didn't raise foolish girls

The Good with the Bad

As I close my eyes, I can remember
Your bruised face in a casket
Your father choking up
As he tried to read Amazing Grace

I can remember your sister calling me
But I can't recall anything she said
Other than "I'm so sorry"
My ears ringing as time stood still

Years later and I still cry
Every time I touch your ashes
But I wear your thumbprint pendant
With so much love and grace

Despite all of the towers you collapsed
I still remember Sunday morning breakfasts
Singing at the top of our lungs on the highway
Standing tall and proud as I stood next to you

Daddy

Anytime I start to miss you
I stare in the mirror
And look at our sleepy eyes
And Grandma Helen's nose

Anytime I start to miss you
I tell an inappropriate joke
And command the entire room
As they fall in stitches

Anytime I start to miss you
I blast Welcome to the Jungle
Alone in my car and attempt
The screeching intro you always nailed

Anytime I start to miss you
I roll a paper or two
Throw on some Bob Marley
And sway in my living room

Anytime I start to miss you
I talk to you out loud
And if I'm lucky,
I'll feel you next to me

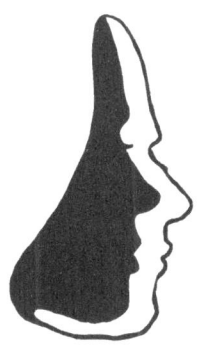

Matriarch

Thank you for breaking your own heart
All those years ago
Mustering the strength each day
To wake up and smile for us

Despite the fact that you were dying
You still showed up everyday
And showed us that you don't
Accept less than what you deserve

No matter how much you love him.
No matter how much you love him.

Integrity

I think you would be really proud
Of the woman I chose to become

Dinner Conversation

I'm sorry for making you cry
And talk about your demons
When you were still fragile
And possessed by all of them

Family is Forever

I'll tell anyone who will listen
That you were such an asshole
But you were our asshole
Behind the moon, beyond the rain

Ab Imo Pectore

Keeper of my deepest secrets
Witness to my childhood
I was the hurricane
You the calm before the storm

I finally started brushing my hair
On the days I absolutely have to
You finally stopped getting grounded
Because you moved out of mom's house

Look how far we've come
Look at everyone we proved wrong
They said we wouldn't amount to much
Assumed we would turn out weak

I would still go to battle for you
Any day of the week
You would still never let me
Fumble through this life alone

They taught us blood is thicker than water
Even if I take my last breath
I'll still be here after death
A bond as viscous as they come

Nephew

My godson's eyes remind me
Men were once little boys
That gives me so much hope
For the ones who still hurt

Resilience

Passing the secret down
Generation to generation
You do what you have to
And you never give up

Wrapping You Into Me

Jesus crying tattooed on your back
Two skulls sat on your shoulder
I have one that I perched on my foot
And wrapped it in green ivy

Conversations with Myself

I forgive you for staying
As long as you did
You made the best decision
You could
With the information you had
At the time

Full

As I sit here writing
Listening to easy music
Mango skin on the bedside table
Dog sprawled out next to me

I feel so full
Content
At peace
Grateful

Insecure Women

I'm not friends with women anymore
That blow out everyone else's candle
So hers can shine the brightest
I'll never fit into a pecking order

Poor Taste

You could hold a diamond
In front of someone for years
But if they prefer silver
That's on them

-Let them

Shipping Out of the East

He said to get out of that town
Where I don't belong to the stuck-up minds
Away from a setting where I'm not appreciated
Move to spaces where I'm a treasure

White Buffalo

I was always too
Good for you
No offense cause
You're a catch too

But I'm just on
A different level
You're going places
But I'm an unstoppable force

Explanation

I think that deep down
You couldn't handle me

And you knew that

You couldn't live with
Letting me down anymore

HBIC

I'm a fucking queen
That should be thriving
At all times

A fair warning for
Anyone getting in my way:
There's the fucking door

A Higher Standard

You were destined for much
Bigger and better things
Than he could've imagined
Don't sell yourself short

Vows to Myself

I promise to be your best friend
Have your best interest always
To be honest no matter how much it hurts
To love and protect you fiercely

The Underdog

Who would've known
That the little girl
From food stamps
And Bristol

Would grow up
To take this world
By the balls
And bring it to its knees

Stay Mad

I warned you elementary bitches
It would be all over for you
Once I started believing in myself
And recognizing my true potential

Drive

I built myself
From the ground up
Started with nothing
What's your excuse?

Facts

It took me a long time
To understand the fact that
It's none of my business
What other people think of me

It only matters what I think of me

Hype Man

If you don't hype yourself up
Believe in yourself 100%
Why should anyone else?

Compliments

Someone told me recently
I have a beautiful soul
I genuinely care when
I ask how they're doing

I try to include everyone
I laugh big and make others laugh
My laugh is contagious
My eye contact inebriating

I'm a treat really
He hates coming home but
I make home feel warm
And that speaks volumes

...I can't remember
The last time someone
Made me feel so
Emotionally naked before

Taking Risks

I would rather fail every day
Trying for the rest of my life
Than to pretend I'm small
And to play it safe

Trailer Park Dreams

Nana tells me about
The 10x40 trailer
She used to cook
Corn beef and cabbage in

She tells me how she
Used to dream she would
Someday make it into
A duplex apartment

She tells me how she
Cried hysterically with a
Baby boy on her hip
Invisible to her first husband

She tells me how she
Got tired of watching him
Climb into a bottle
To find his courage

She tells me how she once
Stood and screamed on top of
A dead man's grave for
Stealing her innocence

She tells me it took her decades
And two more marriages
To find her own voice
Yet she never gave up

She shows me how despite
All of her pain and regrets
You put one foot in front of the other
With a burning courage to love fiercely

Breaking cycles, I am living
Proof of her answered prayers
She reminds me every day that
I come from strong stock

Staying Humble

No matter how much
Success I unearth
I'll always return to
The velvet underground

Loyalty

Any day of the week
I'll always prefer
To slum it
With my day ones

Than to climb
A social ladder
To meet up
With a yuppy

Humanitarian

Everyone deserves to learn
How to believe in themselves
How to heal their wounds
I'm gonna show them how

Natural Hair

You liked my hair best
When it was traditional
Straight, sleek, docile

I like my hair best
When it is unconventional
Wavy, wild, feral

The Alchemist

I transmute my pain into love
Catalyze rejection into triumph
Transfigure anger into joy
Manipulate self-doubt into confidence

Shower

Eyes closed and burning
Water pelts my face
My hands outstretch
Until my finger tips
Feel the pressure
Feel the release
Heaven is already here

A Vibrant Grey

Mercury retrograde had me
In my feelings again
But I'm pushing
Pursuing right through
Learning to relax into it
Learning how to vibe it

Learning to Let Go

You finally admit your truth
You never truly loved yourself
And everything after that
Was destined to fail

You call me a saint
For loving you through it all
Trying to pull you out of a
Hole you refused to surface from

I hope temperance finds you
And serves you well
Your soul deserves inner peace
Your soul deserves your love

We were put into each other's life
To crack open old, karmic wounds
To face our true selves
To raise our consciousness

I'm stepping into the unknown
Unafraid, relaxed, and calm
I'll see you when I see you
Until then, live a good life for me

Compassion

It's hard to hate someone
When you finally understand
Their poor treatment of you
Has nothing to do with you
And everything to do with
How tortured they feel inside

Queen of Swords

A little more truth, a little less you
A lot more confidence, a lot less deception
I know what these bones are made of
What this song is supposed to sing

Confusion quartz to clarity
A sword strikes a stone
The sky claps and lights the black
I am the eye of the storm

Taking my losses as wins
Leaving you in that sentimental terminal
Taking flights to new horizons
Open my pinions before you can clip them

You'll be a line on a page
All in due time
I'm already feeling bored
When they speak your name

Turtle Dove Hauntings

The words drip from your lips
Effortlessly into my ears
You miss me
Expecting an open embrace
Upon your revelations

Do not ask of me
If the feeling is mutual
As you will be disappointed
I am incapable of feeling
A loss for you

Yet, I am not a lake
That has droughted to desert
Turtle dove hauntings happen
Let me begin to describe
The losses I yearn for

I missed giggling uncontrollably
Feeling powerful and confident
Speaking my veracity loudly
Void of stammered speech
A life full of faith and truth

I missed trusting in the wind
Feeling her abundance and grace
Walking tall with her at my back
Grounding me to the earth
Allowing me to know who I am

I missed my wildly passion
Unbridled ambition and dreams
The magic that coursed my blood
Optimism breeding hope and courage
Compassed intuition allowing me to see

Do not ask of me
If the feeling is mutual
You belittled and sequestered
The gifts of which brought me life
Essence you futilely tried to pilfer

Synaptic Cleft Diffusion

Bread crumb trails lead me into darkness
Temptation to fall down the rabbit hole
Yearning to sedate my grief fully
A risk my emotions want to take

Yet, here I am, standing alone
My tongue lost the taste for Panko
I place a hand to my lower abdomen
That holds half of my future child

Her future hangs in my hands
Every action produces consequence
So, I step away from falling in
I let my grief wash over me fully

Another dance with the devil
Isn't worth a lifetime of hell
I stop my impulse and muscle memory
Cause to love her, is to love myself

Sorrow & Joy

How lucky am I
To be able to
Hold my broken heart
With a smile on my face

Tears in my eyes
Because I was blessed
With years of loving you
How lucky am I?

Wine Haze

Boxes pack up my shit
But memories stay etched
Can't seem to erase you
Despite my valiant efforts

My new home holds such hope
Yet I cried leaving you behind
Sometimes a wine haze helps
Other times, your absence stings

Learning to hold the spaces
In which I still love you
Simultaneously moving forward
They keep saying there will be better days

Wishing you were standing here with me
Making new memories, living our life
But I'm safer doing this alone
I'm healthier standing on my own

My lips cup against the glass
Eyes closed and I wonder about you
I'm just trying to find my way
Without you in the way

Wounded but Dancing

I still feel sad every now and then
I know I could get you back if I tried
But given the choice, I'll choose myself
Over and over and over again

Spring

The snow began to thaw
The wind stopped stinging
The birds began to chirp
I can't help but feel rebirthed too

Feeling Good as Hell

I've seen the growth in me
I am one strong ass
Powerful woman
And it shows everyday

iii. Tests, Allies, Enemies

Still Healing

Another memory floats back
Into the present moment
She waited for you to come
But you left her waiting

Dove cries and wings wounded
She becomes blind to her worth
Forgets the day on those steps
But carries a fear of abandonment

Grief sequestered
Cries and pain pushed aside
She learns to suture her own wounds
She does not know how to nurture her heart

Lonely child, where are your protectors?
My green eyes match hers
She quivers and shrugs
Her pain all too familiar

I tell her she is valuable
She has always been treasured
I will protect her because
I can finally protect myself.

Out of the Tree of Life

You think you're happy now?
Just wait a little bit

The best is yet to come

Full Integration

I remember feeling as though
The tears would never stop coming

I now wear these scars proudly
And my green eyes are still kind

Authenticity and love consolation prizes
For walking the land of the dead

But I've finally rounded the corner
And I can't stop laughing and smiling

Useless Vices

I tried to roll it away in papers
That would burn one down
But a moment of numbness
Never lasts for long

I tried to find solace
In a new stranger's arms
But everyone has carry-ons
Full of baggage

I tried to quench my thirst
Drowning my sorrows
But it just burned my throat
The hangovers filled with grief

I tried to work it away
Find purpose in busyness
But that widened my loneliness
Filling minutes with diligent work

I tried to sweat it out
Stretch my body to its limits
But I couldn't escape myself
I couldn't run away

Every time I sit in a wave of emotion
It always passes
Resistance builds more tension
Blocking manifestation

Every wave I endure
I come out more confident
That I can handle anything
And everything thrown my way

Trigger Part One.

Years later. She finally asks.
What you did to me.
As if she asked.
What is my favorite color.

As if my sexual assault.
Is simple small talk.

When my therapist asks me
"What does it feel like?"
It feels like you're
Still violating me

Inside of me.
As if you never stopped
Penetrating me

My body tight. My breath short.
Bracing myself through the motions.

Trigger Part Two.

Breaking down on a sunny afternoon
Screaming into a shower wall
Falling water beautifully
Pattering the ground

Sex became easy.
Sexual intimacy became impossible.
You violated sacred union
You muddied spiritual beauty

You made my body a prison
Somatization and fear
All I want is to trust
The man I make love to

You made my body a prison
All I want is to go home
You made my body a prison
All I need is to be seen.

But I like to hide
In broad daylight.

What's your favorite color?

To the First Man That Loved Me

You want to love every inch of me
You want to see every corner of my soul
You want to kiss the wounds left by others
You want to hold my tired, scared bones

I want to let you see the depths of me
I want to let you love me in my entirety
I want to allow you to see me
I want to lay down these walls

But I can't.
I'm trying so hard.
I'm just not there yet.
I'm sorry.

Underground World

My speech and aura draw you closer
Curiosity tickling your interest
Met with suspicion and confusion
You don't find me intimidating

What others consider intense
You consider a breath of fresh air
What others consider perverse
You consider to be peculiar

You draw in closer and closer
Eyeing through various veils
You see through the walls
Inching closer and closer to center

Appreciating and acknowledging my beauty
But shoveling through my depths
You find an underground world
Full of wonder and fascination

A guest in my inner world,
You watch and learn what makes it tick
Unwavering in the films of my past
You bear witness and hold me tight

You look at me with such adoration
I've never been loved like this
This must be what safety feels like
You're the first one to see, me.

Hope

I stopped believing in
Fairytales years ago

But you,

You might be the one
To break the spell

My Well-Being Is More Important
Than Your Happiness

It's quite true,
I've fallen for you

But I will always
Love myself more

The Last Leg

Toxic energy is loosened
And floats through my body
Looking for a way out
I take a deep inhale

Through the exhale
Through the mental fog
I hold firm in myself
This too shall pass

First Breath

I'm told the body keeps score
Although I've processed
I've found compassion
I've found forgiveness

It is stuck in my muscles
Like a sailor's knot
Stuck on a 30-year-old buoy
Floating underneath the surface

Ears ringing as the triggers come
Letting them flood in
What washes in, will wash away
One last storm to clear the land

One last gust of wind
To push the tides violent
To shake up what has settled
On the bottom ocean floor

With the turbulence
The knots shall loosen
Around my ankles
As I kick to the surface

Eyes still closed
My face feels the salt air
I never realized how long
I was holding my breath for.

Summer Love

You adored my wild hair
Feral waves
You don't want to tame me
So you set me free

Hell of a Run

You find safety in logic
Safety in your own plans
You didn't plan on
Falling in love with me

I appeared and illuminated
Your world and tunneled
Underneath your skin
Your logic losing rationale

I made you feel to depths
And you chose your safety
And your threatening woman
Sits a world away now

Watching a Bajan sunset
I wonder what you see
In your desert sky tonight
More so, what you try to ignore

If I close my eyes, the warm air
Can feel like your voice in my ear
If I fall asleep and dream hard enough
I can lie in your arms a few hours more

When Love Brings Healing

What was wild and true
Never quite got off the ground
Feeling love unfinished
We decide to leave it alone

Maybe you'll change your mind
Maybe this was just a simple lesson
I'm grateful for the opportunity
To love you something fierce and senseless

Thank you for showing me men are good
Men are gentle, kind, loving, and honest
I'll forever hold your memory alive
Inside my heart, a sincere love

Destiny Is A Funny Thing

If you wake up in the middle of the night
And notice foot prints in your dream clouds
It was just me, passing through
Walking across your deepest thoughts

And I sift my finger in a bowl of charms
Trying to find some new luck
But all I want is to sit in your arms
Universe surrender mouthing, "what the fuck."

Do you close your eyes and see mine?
I see you everywhere I look
You're tunneled into my DNA
Encoding new memories and habits

I think of you every hour and I wonder
What adventure you're on now
You stirred my soul awake
I yearn to peak and blossom out loud

A fearful girl became a fearless woman
A fulsome, gracious juggernaut
You showed me what I should be
And wouldn't you know, the shoe fits.

Wild, Wonderful, Weightless

I know her manipulation and shame games too well
Mother dearest, mother fiercest
Wrapped, fragile identity into others
Fragile like a bomb

Push and pull, black and white
Love and hate, back and forth
Judgement falls from her lips
In an effort to control my spirit

While she slept on me
I dissected her shadows from mine
Attached her to a decoy
I can slip in and out of

When she wakes to see that I have
Fled the coup for self-preservation
She will accuse me of being wild, terrible, and selfish
A dragon will pretend to be a maimed waif

Licking her wounds for attention
I've resurrected my essence
Wouldn't you know I'm gaining momentum
She can't stop me. She can't touch me.

When It's Over

I've been here before
I let myself simply be
Maybe with age you learn
To let go of denial

I let the pain come
I let the pain go
Oscillating through waves
I simply float on my back

If you saw the state I'm in
You'd tell me to get my shit together
But I'm left to my own devices
Whether or not you like it

Archangel Orion

Orion shows me lavender flames
I receive it in open palms
Playing a movie of my past
I stand in the hall of Akashic records

Everything has a point, a purpose
I look to the future picture
But it blurs out
Focus on the present open tablet

A translucent scribe pushes from the shelf
I gaze and watch a glowing heart inside
He tells me to apply flame to the scribe
Release and free the heart inside

Release and free the heart inside
Release and free the heart inside
Release and free your heart inside
Release and free your heart inside

Dragon

Visions of flames haunt me
I feel blockages burning off
Incinerating all that no longer serves
It all served a purpose at a point in time

Don't you see child?
You are the weapon of the universe
You are forged from the flames
You were born in the fire

Don't you see child?
You cannot be destroyed
Ember glow lipping my feet
I make amends with the heat

No more resisting steam pressure
I am the weapon of the universe
I am forged from the fire
I am indestructible.

Conquistador

I decided to lie down next to my anger
To understand her plight of war
I wanted to understand her severity
I wanted to understand her purpose

Who was this momentum of energy?
That has tortured and inspired me?
What was she looking for?
Conquistador burning towns and cities

What will finally quench her thirst?
What will simmer her angst?
What will bring her eternal peace?
What will break the wild Mustang?

Protective armor stabbing the inside out
Her insides numb and detached from her nerves
She turns the pain inside out
Bellowing into the dark night

The villages prepare to sedate the beast
But she only grows in size
She shows me visions of her operation
In a constant search for missing parts

What is an empress without her heart?
What is a hierophant without solitude?
She tells me to find her stolen inner light
Light that abolishes century agony

To find my light is to find my love
To find my love is to find my compassion
To find compassion is to find forgiveness
To find forgiveness is to find eternal peace

Gifting Myself

Hurt child lost in the shuffle
Bright green eyes welled and wet
Confusion and stifled wailing
A pawn in a parental chess game

Tit for tat, get ahead mentality
Stepfather, stepmother, stepped life
Home ripped wide open
Don't blink, everything will change

Weird and twisted emotions covered
Decades of sleeping
Here I am, awake alas
Picking open the scabs

If I cannot find love
I will love myself
If I cannot find nurturance
I will nurture myself

If I cannot find peace
I will give myself peace
If I cannot find safety
I will gift myself freedom

If I cannot find apologies
I will heal myself
If I cannot find acceptance
I will gift myself approval

Open

Manifesting thoughts and honors
Your worrisome head alight
Feeble attempt at castration
You are the divine masculine within

You cannot renounce or reject
What you are at the core
Yin and yang exist in your soul
Duality is the balance you seek

You child are the ticket to rejoice
You are built for your journey
Trust, the universe has much to offer
All you need is an open hand and heart

Nobility

I thought you were noble and kind
Honest and true to your integrity
All I see is a meek, scared boy
Step aside so the empress can walk by

She Wolf

Cross legged, bare skin and surrendered
Eyes closed to sanctity
Uncombed hair reflecting emotions
Empty her, fill her, she is a conduit

A wolf in the night
Moving in silence
Who are the crazy ones?
Her actions speak of themselves

She accentuates her mind
Acknowledging various binds
Snipping the knots loose
Slipping away during the night

She will rise
She will come
She will rise
She will stand

A Choice

She may still hold her aching chest
Tears may rain down her cheeks
She may think of you often
But there is no haste

Sand has taught her grace
Pain catalyzed into lessons
If given the choice
She will choose herself.

Shadow

My father taught me how to lie without blinking
My mother taught me how to destroy cities with my tongue

He taught me boundaries are meaningless
She taught me survival equates ruthlessness

He taught me how to be callously selfish by example
Her example left me groveling for love & acceptance

These toxic lessons waltz and haunt the dark corners of me
Effortless, commanding, mindless. The beat hums

Unconscious self-imposed oppression
A goat head laughs

Further into the abyss I fall
Collecting scars and scorn

I pull myself out of the dark ballroom
Where my skeletons don't hide, they dance

Unspoken

Red paper plates line a table
Empty, lifeless, sterile
Appearances on display
Facades freckling truth

Standstill and quiet
She expects too much
None of herself
Tangled in hope and lies

Guises of nurturance
True selves rotting flesh
I need to escape from her
Before she irreversibly infects me

The Love is Still There

The sound of your voice awakens
The things I've tried to put to bed
I can't help myself
I allow them to tip toe back

Into my heart, to feel it once more
My head warns me I'm flirting with pain
I can pretend for a moment or two
The world belongs to us again

Graceful Encore

A bird cawing symphony
Underneath the canopy
Golden hour glow kissing my skin
Eyes closed and I lift my chin
Listening to off key winged song
Content moment consequently long
Transmuted waves of chaos in a calm sea
Spectating crows dance among the leaves
Serum rubbed into scars that are fading
A life well lived no longer in waiting
Spaces found for free spirits to roam
Impounded impulses lifted out of bones
Breath filled lungs with gratitude
Liberation won through latitude
Have you ever seen a day so beautiful before?
Have you ever ushered in a graceful encore?

Dandelion Vice

A half corpse bumble bee
Sipping his final pollen
The first frost causing
Weakened wings, a slowed pulse

Letting what he loves kill him
Instead of seeking safe shelter
Savoring those last moments
On petals of his sweet dandelion

Boxed Hope

Incomprehensible flowered love that sailed in silently
Whisked away in the wind, tears make fading colors soften

A final warm sunset and she tries to swallow her dried throat
Living in an orange and red leaf painted world now

Her sorrow tucked neatly in a box with his name on it
Contemplation of incinerating its contents

She can't stomach being responsible for a thorough murder
Hope is a son of a bitch.

Whistleblower

Silent tears, invisible scars shoveled
From the grave of family secrets

A tired soul greased the whistle well
Puffed her cheeks as pressured as she could

Unwillingness to slowly die
For outward appearances

Cleansed hands of toxic sap
That keeps feet and growth stagnant

Snapping the devices and tactics
That keep self-love hard to reach

Trimmed to Restrain

A young child asked her mother why her pet bird
Wouldn't attempt to fly away to its freedom

She simply answered the impressionable child
Keep their wings clipped so they fall mid flight

Premonition of fate for the uninhibited child
Who didn't comprehend her own free spirit yet

Unbeknownst to the mother, escape was child's destiny
Baby bird willed the skies open under her wings

I'll Break Any Chair You
Attempt to Tie Me To

Your fears won't prevent me
From tasting ripened fruit

Your guilt won't stop me from
Climbing in and out of steep canyons

Loving reckless men thoroughly
Until I break my own heart

Walking unscathed into war zones
Until I earn massive scars

I want my knees skinned and
Legs bruised from dancing

Wrinkles around my mouth
From laughing and smiling

I want to live disastrously
I want to live fully

I want to know how differently
The air tastes in foreign lands

I want to know world wonders
From first-hand experience

I want to be larger than life
I want to feel *everything*

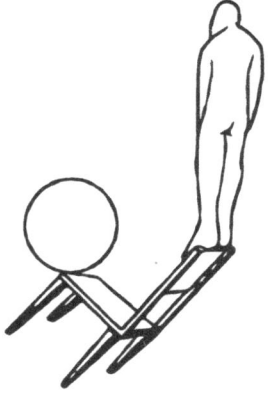

Bones

Structured but dilapidated
Some corners whittled sharp
Some whittled blunt
Marrow a reservoir for meals

Stacked skulls lining a shelf
Impersonation immortalized
Cold and clawed with teeth marks
A piece easily weaponized

Lovely and porcelain
I stretch mine out
To touch what remains
Chunks among ash in an urn

Unforgiving and broken
Recognizable pained limp
Clutching onto crutches
Afraid to rely on design

Flesh opens and erodes
What remains underneath
Reveals what we're made of
Will the house stand or fall?

Emotional Abuse

Stockholm syndromed synergy slides through
Empathy and emotional intelligence perused
You yell your yielding an articulate truth
Yet your yeanling deems it uncouth

Harking the contrast, she comes up for air
Meeting a hand covered blowhole snare
Legs thrashing, face turning blue-gray
Mouth corner smiles watching panicked airway

Extracting her to safety as terror preludes
An act which endows immediate gratitude
Air fills her exhausted lungs, watered down
Hiding perturbation of almost letting her drown

Gaslighting

You downplay your emotional violence
Gaslighting me at every turn
Undermining my truth and feelings
Claiming my memory is unfortunate

Survival

You expected me to be there for you as the parent
The nurturance you were so cruelly deprived of
I was your egotistic supply, the golden child
You knew to keep me emotionally lean, hungry

Isolated and trusting, you gave me breadcrumbs of safety
And the appreciation on my face validated your worth
Keeping me dependent, kept you safe, made you important
You saw so much of yourself in me, you always said

You perfected the ability to keep me hungry, needing you
But you never learned to control my willpower, could you?
Something always reflected back to you, didn't it?
Always reminding you of all you would and could never be.

Oscillating your emotions very finely between love and hate
How selfish of me to break free and become my own person
You needed me sick and small to keep you well and afloat
I always knew, deep down, this was not normalcy

As I search the world to find my place and my truth
You feel your nail grip weaken and weaken
Starved of supply, you curse my individuality
What kind of monster would let their kin starve?

My Father's Hands

I'm at peace with who you were
Everything you were not

I know the dark thoughts and the
Darker actions you inflicted

The coals of anger weren't mine
To hold onto anymore

With these scars, I stretch my palms
Deep breaths, I feel you here with me

Not everyone else understands that
I love you unconditionally, still

All Here.

Sitting still in the silence of discomfort
Passing nonjudgment to thoughts of suffer
Being all here. Being all here now.
This is the alcove where healing allows

Don't push yourself out and retreat
Sit here...sit inside the grief
Trace the wounds with your fingers
Only your touch can heal what lingers

Sit with your tired, weary bones
Beautiful ivory magnificence you own
Lay down next to your vulnerability
Whisper your secrets in tranquility

This is the moment you find strength
This is where you find final length
Breathe in and out of it. Feel the sting.
But you're still inhaling despite everything

Despite it all, you're still inhaling
You're still laughing despite ailing
You're still dancing despite flaws
You're still here, despite it all

All here.

Nauseous

Disconnecting and dissecting
The root of your codependency
Nauseating reality
What's a family, really.

Self-Doubt

She's afraid love will always be difficult
Elusive, a figment of her own imagination
They all leave eventually, don't they?
Discouraged to be the common denominator

Too loud. Too independent. Too wild.
Too free to keep and hold onto. Too much.
A bird conditionally loved as much as
Her willingness to be caged and owned

No choice but to lean into her nature
Afraid, they say she's difficult to love.
Different. Divergent. Desolate. Distinct.
What if the rumors are true? What if they're right?

Contrasting and armored, she closes her eyes
Who are you, you indigenous creature?
What are you, you vehement drifter?
Temperament incapable of being assuaged

She's not a thing to be assimilated, my love
Only the brave ones with piqued curiosity
And an admiration for a tameless spirit
Could be strong enough to love her

Horse Shoe

Instinct overwhelming intellect
She feels, she feels, how she feels
Surely, there is someone, that desires
A pace of one thousand horse hooves

Gratitude

I finally unclench my fists, nails imbedded into my palms
Pain viscous and justified, hissing anger permeating
As my fingers open, exposing my bleeding palms
I let your past transgressions fall to the ground

And as we hear them shatter upon impact
My eyes become wet as I look into those blue greens
I see all the reasons I loved you in the first place
Gratitude for you and your lessons wash over my body

That's when I knew I had finally forgiven you
And as we wish each other well at this bifurcation
A poignant goodbye, released from chains of guilt
Bittersweet memories of us are all I need to take

Vowel.

You're the basic speech sound
Which makes my breath partially obstructed
Combined with me, a harmony

I am the speech sound which is an
Open configuration in your throat
A vibration within your vocal cords

I am the inaudible friction
A unit of the sound system
From which forms the nucleus of language

Human.

Extending my empathy like branches
Slowly budding and rising
To touch those whom
Have hacked my limbs

We know not what we do
But I am brave enough
To offer forgiveness to
Those who are simply human

I'm Not God

Who am I to deny someone forgiveness?
We all are deserving of compassion
We are not defined by our sins
All saints are sinners, after all

A Love Letter to Everyone
Who Has Hurt Me, Including Myself

Losing the lenses of judgment
I see how much pain you carry
As benevolence arises out of my chest
I long to hold your face in my hands

And tell you how perfect you are
Did you forget how infectious your laughter is?
Did you deny yourself love and turn on yourself?
Did you react out of fear and abandonment?

I long to embrace your tired bones
And hold a mirror to your beauty
Remind you of all the good you gave me
Remind you of all you are yet to be

I long to wash and comb out the knots
In your hair, tangled in grief
I long to listen to your story
I long for your pain to be seen

And as we rake your grief and disappointment
I long to make you strong enough
To pull yourself back up, for yourself
To find grace and forgiveness, for yourself

I long to make you brave enough
To face your own dancing demons
To take shelter within your spirit
When the waves come knocking for you

I long to wipe the tears from your eyes
So you can see how fear is an illusion
You have so much worth beyond your agony
Beckoning you to stand in your power

You are a disastrous combustion of experiences
Yet here you still are, all here. Beautiful.
Life has been incapable of wiping out your flame
Let it glow. Let it glow.

I love you.

Leaning Out of Anger

I thought that walls and condemnation
Would protect me from further hurt
Keeping those who are flawed
In a demonizing light

I thought being the victim
Meant I was justified in my anger
Allowed me to do whatever, to whoever
I was the wrath to be feared

In creating fear in their hearts
I felt powerful for once
Blind that negativity breeds negativity
I, hurt, no more powerful than them

I found my power in forgiveness
I found protection in forging peace
I found love in boundaries
I found compassion for everyone

Connectedness is the human experience
In which will propel us forward
Love for your neighbor
Love for those who condemn you

We are all longing for relation
A hunger for genuine connection
To be seen and heard. Appreciated.
There are no such things as mistakes.

Letting It Go

Let's move on
And simply live
Love
Breathe

Latte Thoughts

I want to know what I can do
To leave this place
Better than I found it

Blood Thicker Than Water

This is how we're going to heal
I'm going to love you
Unconditionally
Hold space for you

While you figure it out
I believe in you
In your ability to overcome
We're going to be a family again

Someday. Someway.

Tasked

A reflected pink sunset
Dealing with reality
How you focus
Building with integrity

Giving

Grateful for growth
Love for your home
Heart on the table
Infinite servings

They say a blessing
Prior to the devour
Satiated palates
For the first time.

The Message

Opening my book wide open
Terrorizes me
Until I saw
They needed the words

In Loving Memory

That song keeps playing over and over in my head
        "I think it's cause I remember for the first time,
            Since I hated you, that I used to love you"
Wiping my wet cheeks, I remember the love we once had

Learning

Contrary to popular belief
You don't have to hate someone
You used to love dearly
In order to move on with your life

A Prayer

I pray your daughter teaches you
Everything you need to know
About loving a woman

I pray your wife shows you
Mothers can and should nurture
And be a respite in this world

I pray you learn that femininity is not
Meant to be conquered and overpowered
But cherished, protected and adored

I pray you find it in your heart to
Forgive the feminine that filleted you
Open as a small, defenseless boy

I pray you come to learn that we
Are here to soothe your fears
Break your oppression from affection

I pray she opens your heart and fills
Your cup with compassion, tenderness
Gentleness and kindness and love

    I pray she heals your heart
    I pray you feel deserving
    I pray you feel worthy

Reminisce

When you hear EC's "Springsteen"
Do you think about being nineteen?
Summer events turned timeless memories
A hot night temper without any remedy

Do you think of our good old friend,
John Daniels and the time spent with him
Talks for hours that never seemed to end
Headaches he gave us to try and mend

When you watch 4th of July fireworks
Do you think of Dallas veteran perks
Texas air not the only thing filled with sparks
Burning each joint down and leaving a mark

When you hear New Haven's name
Do you think of SCSU football games
Talking back in your dorm all afternoon
Or my lips on yours in a locked bar bathroom

Maybe your pompous brother was right all along
Together, the world would burn, simply wrong
Kindred spirits but terrible partners
But my god were we the perfect lovers

When I think of you I want to remember
All the good in the last ten years
All the passion and excess in love
All the times we laughed until we cried

Time has come to finally grow up
But somewhere in time, we're still
Those two wild kids that just knew they
Were madly in love and finally acted on it

Thank You.

We were witnesses to
The best parts of us

A light so blinding
It illuminated

All of the shadows
Unwilling to come forth

Burning its skin, we set
Each other in agonizing fire

A touch that debrides wounds
Painful yet healing

Coal squeezed into
Unruly pressure

It made me who I am
Thank you.

Denying the Impulse

Every ounce in my bones wants to jump ship
Press my feet into the ground
Never looking over my shoulder
Disillusionment

If I can't learn to swim
Amongst the most personal
Of sharks
In familiar waters

What good will I be
At paddling my limbs
In an unfamiliar sea
In unknown depths

Last Leg

Running around the corner
Three quarters of the way
My legs start to quiver
But I push, push, push.

Vellum.

Your skin is not a home for beggars
Or a hostel for vagabonds

Tumbleweeds driven by wind
Scattering seeds to beyond

Drinking you fast to forget
Pacifying sorrow and regret

Hands that touch your bare skin
Transferring paralyzed agony

You are a relic to be venerated
Reincarnated truth to be sipped slowly

Let his legs tremble in your presence
Witnessing the strength of your power

Bring him to his knees in awe
Of your beauty and divinity

If he who dares to bow before you
Shall esteem you as his deity

Let his heart be as loyal
As the tides to the moon

Let his strength be balanced
With vulnerability and truth

May he fuel your passions
May he quench your dry throat

You, my dear, are not a lodge
For cheap, reckless men

You, my dear, are a sanctuary
To be held by gallant, gentle gods

Exposed.

Your heart is not a meal
For souls with emaciated mouths

But if placed on a platter
May it spoil to venom

So, as it touches marauder lips
It turns malevolent insides out

Obscure.

You are the epitome of tenacity
Flipping concepts on their head

You are the pinnacle of intensity
Riveting what is stagnant in the dark

With an angelic and tender heart
You feel to depths most can't see

You have electricity pulsing
Through your being, forced to stand out

You are the hero and love interest
Of your own arduous story

With your piercing half crescent eyes
They are blind to your vast softness

You are equal parts darkness and light
Through imperfections you are flawless

You are live wire passion
Disastrous but full hearted

With animalistic tendencies you revel
In your nature rather than your nurture

You are hellion and fire
Water and sustenance

You are too intricate and great
To be confined to one narrative

Becoming Authentic.

The greater your light
The darker your shadow

Don't deny your parts
Call them by their names

It is when we fear and
Attempt to quell our nature

That we live in disharmony
Becoming an inauthentic self

Knowing the depths of your night
Allows for knowing its own cure

Only you can soothe inner beasts
They can only recognize your voice

Starving them from attention is what
Causes them to eventually turn on you

So feed them, love them, know them and
Watch yourself grow into your authenticity

Alpha.

Quelling the beast
That was once a cub

Teaching her to walk away
From those who persecute

Instead of lunging for
Their unprotected throats

Showing her how inner peace
Overrules a need for justice

Those who protect your head
Those who shield your heart

Will never come to as long as
You wear your foe's blood

On your mouth like lipstick
Their teeth strung in a necklace

You are regal, you are an heiress
Unlock your jaw, show them mercy

Diaphragm Movements

You are not your thoughts.
You are not your emotions.

You are not your ego.
You are not your reputation.

Breathe in. Observe.
Breathe out. Appreciate.

You are not your impulses.
You are not your nerves.

You are not your mistakes.
You are not your accomplishments

Breathe in. Witness it all.
Breathe out. Let it go.

You Belong to You

You have been shared and passed around
Like a platter full of hors d'oeuvres

Like an endless supply of wine
Drunken by insatiable thirsts

Of course you don't yet feel
As though you belong to you

Keep choosing yourself baby girl
You have always belonged to you

Learning to Trust Myself Again

You were never taught to memorize your flesh
You were never taught to love your archetype

You needed a parent to soothe your cries
But you learned to bite your bottom lip

Dismiss your tangled emotions as such
Analyze and discuss them instead

You're not comfortable in your own head
You have sought refuge in other's arms

For such a careless and feral little girl
You sure have come further than anyone thought

Envy falls from their lips to see a struggle
Turned itself into a masterpiece effortlessly

Rest at this passing a moment longer
Consume yourself into your essence

Walk out of these canyons emerged
Like a butterfly off of a flower

Grace is your birthright my love
Don't you see how wonderful you are?

Most of All

You're an impulsive chest tattoo while
Out of town for professional development

You're a 1 am serenade in a
Bourbon street karaoke bar

You're a scraped bleeding leg
From climbing stone walls in Tempe

You're a genial conversation
With strangers in Barbados

You're dancing feet and swaying
Hips on top of a catamaran

You're screams of delight and fear
Zip lining through jungle canopies

You're a shotgun and shit talk
When you hang with old friends

You're unpredictably timed dark humor
Smiling when everyone else looks horrified

You're a target hard to shoot down
Forever moving and searching

You're a coquettish tease
Bedroom eyes and a demure smile

Most of all

You're a soft, safe place to land
For the ones you hold in your heart

Mycorrhizal Network

Branches tranquil, trunks stable
Silent observers, unassuming guards

Beneath the thick earth is an
Underground fungal organization

Webbing out for miles below
Warning of imminent danger

These inconspicuous spies
Cloak my feet into their roots

Apart of the clandestine grid
Telling me everything

Solace.

Energy heightened, I can't breathe
Bombarded thoughts on top of thoughts

Worn-out from the constant plug in
My access too simply obtained

My verve belongs to me and me alone
Deep longing to be disconnected

From everyone and everything
That drains and decelerates me

I find my solace in true silence
Galaxy where the ego can't exist

My lungs fill fully in peace
I dissolve into the stillness

Bristol

They bulldozed a childhood home
Sweet bitterness bites my tongue

Longing for a backyard swing set
Longing for the quiet before the storm

I can feel the wind in my hair still
As my eyes close as I kick my legs

Higher and higher and higher
Gravity pulls me down to the earth

And you pulled me into your chest
You held me. You loved me.

A wrinkle in time reminds me
You were nurturing at one point

Broken Vow of Silence

My lungs can't catch the air
I'm trying to breathe
But no matter how deep I
Inhale, they can't fully fill

Where do I put this anger?
Where do I put this hurt?
Where do I put this trauma?
Where do I put this shame?

Rendered completely voiceless
I've kept my promise of silence
Let you go on and live your life
While your actions live inside me

How many times did I tell you no?
How many times did your needs
Outrank mine?
How many times was sex your tool
To control my tameless spirit?

How many times did I try to run
Far away from you
How many times did you stalk me
Like your prey

How many times did you pick me up
When I was drunk, wasted, annihilated
Told me I shouldn't drive home
I could crash at your place tonight

You then proceeded to fuck me
When I could not give consent
As I lied in your bed
How many times did it happen

How many times did you scream in
My fucking face to scare me
Did you feel like a fucking man
Banging on my car windows

Screaming to open the fucking door
Snot running down my face
Red faced, crying and covering my head
Pleading for you to leave me alone?

How about when you lied to my face
To get back into my good graces
After my father died hours before
Taking advantage of my vulnerability

But no. I'm the bad guy now.
Because I broke my vow of silence
I stopped letting your actions
Live inside my tissues

Letting you knot my back
Somatization causing fugue
Causing emotional pain to
Finally be physical
To eternally punish me

That's what you wanted?
Isn't it?
To break me? To watch the life
Get sucked right out of me?

Guess what motherfucker.
I'm still fucking here.
You didn't break me.
You fucking made me.

And I'm just getting started.

Classic

I wrote a script as
My client told me
His opiate withdrawal
Symptoms. Classic.

Running nose.
Body aches.
Vomiting.
Diarrhea.

I remember you ate
Egg drop soup
It was all you could stomach
You said you had the flu

A child believes everything
Their parents tell them
You lied. You forced yourself
To withdraw in front of us

Instead of disappearing
And using again
You hurt yourself
For hurting us

My Truth

I can't keep quiet anymore.
I can't be eaten alive.
No matter who it upsets
No matter who it offends

You abused me.
That is not opinion.
That is not debatable.
That is my truth.

Empty

Flat tires on the two back wheels
I self-sabotaged and stabbed
Them impulsively myself

I tried driving back to love

But it was forgiveness that
Was fueling the tank
And well, I was empty.

Cocoon Awakening

While I slept inside my cocoon of pain
Anger kept a vigilant watch
As I opened my eyes one day
I saw the destruction she caused

What have you done?

Self-Righteous

I was impatient. Hurting.
I didn't know how to forgive
Held you captive in your guilt
Punished you over and over again

Made you a slave to your mistakes
Shrunk you down to size
I made my arms shards of glass
That impaled you when you embraced me

I called it self-preservation
I locked my vulnerability away
Far from you, so you couldn't see
Self-righteous and self-sabotaging

I had the best of intentions
I hope in time you can forgive me
For my callous, cold ways
For my detachment from love

Shared Blame

It wasn't all your fault.

Nail in the Coffin

Lovers swaying to and forth
Driving all night to find
Each other's arms again
Only to keep missing one another

Universe keeping them apart
They test fate time and again
Mistake after mistake
It's finally too late

My Chest Hurts

I'm addicted to skin
Yearning and needing mine

I'm addicted to his
Fleeting surface attention

I'm addicted to the idea
Of being needed and loved

I'm addicted to pain
I'm addicted to chaos

I was lonely and sad
He made me laugh

I convinced myself he
Was not a pacifier for grief

But the band aid is ripped
And I'm still in love with you

I'm so sorry. I'm so sorry.
I'm so sorry. I'm so sorry.

Myself Only

I'm ready to start speaking out loud
About the things you did to me
In dark bedrooms and houses

The things that live inside my marrow
Things so heavy that they
Weigh me down and pin me to the floor

The floor with coolness that kissed
My cheek as I lied there defeated
Pretending I was somewhere else

The hands I used to cover my head
In horror, locked in my own car
Hearing your pounding fists on the windows

The hot, desperate tears that fell
As you disassembled me into a
Million puzzle pieces

The emptiness I felt
The apathy I felt
Towards myself

The twisted reflection you created
So I was unrecognizable in a mirror
Trusted you to tell me who it was

The cyborg you made out of me
That refused to cooperate
That continually malfunctioned

My essence could never be tamed
Nor molded into your vision
For I have always belonged to myself

And myself only.

Play

Let's play a little game, shall we?
I'll tell you a fantasy of mine
Since I made all of yours come true

I fantasize swinging a bat to
Your screaming, open mouth
I gleefully take delight in your pain

I romanticize the sound of impact
Of wood meeting your porcelain teeth
The sweetest music to my ears

I daydream seeing the blood drip
From your mouth and down your chin
Don't forget to smile, my love

I dream of picking your teeth out of
The barrel, handing them back to you
I try to be as conscientious as I can be

I long to make your head a house of horrors
As you so kindly did to mine years ago
Do unto others as you wish to be done to you

When Your Rape Isn't Violent

Your needs above mine
Self-betrayal, on my knees
I drank jack and cokes
You drank my bare skin

You didn't hold me down
I didn't kick and scream
Violated, dark boundaries painted
In soft, pretty pastels of honey

He raped me.
He raped me.
He raped me.
He raped me.
He raped me.
He raped me.
He raped me.
He raped me.
He raped me.
He raped me.
He raped me.
He raped me.
He raped me.
He raped me.
He raped me.
He raped me.
He raped me.
He raped me.
He raped me.
He raped me.
He raped me.
He raped me.
He raped me.
He raped me.
He raped me.
He raped me.
He raped me.
He raped me.
He raped me.
He raped me.
He raped me.
He raped me.
He raped me.
He raped me.
He raped me.
He raped me.
He raped me.
He raped me.
He raped me.
He raped me.
He raped me.
He raped me.
He raped me.
He raped me.
He raped me.

And I Endured.

iv. Return With the Elixir

Am I Angry At My Father or My Lover

I saw my first shooting star
They ran across the sky
Void of light pollution
I made endless wishes

I believed in your ability
To answer my prayers
Admiring each other from
Our pedestals we stood on

You promised me the world
Showed me glimpses of
What my life could be
You were my everything and all

Rome wasn't built in a day
But it was destroyed in one
You left me alone to
Climb out of the rubble

Now I can't sleep because
I'm afraid of having dreams
Darkness comforts me because
At least she's consistent

You were an ember glow
That kept my warm soul
But you destroyed my safety
Burning it down with you

I became the nomad that
Passes through and smiles
But befriends no one
Certainly, never stays

The Hedonist

She used to be a masochist, a narrow line
    between pleasure and pain
Hung on your every word, dreamt a life in
    nonexistent colors
Small, unknown to herself, she loved your
    exuberance and excess
Although, your tireless pleasure seeking broke her in
    half

Unknowingly, you busted her wide open into herself
She felt it, something shifted. Something changed
She tried to stay small, stay inside her cracked shell
Tried to tell herself you were enough to love forever

She could no longer cower in the corner for camouflage
An outgrown shell is crushed by the weight of who she is
    to become
There is no denying she is the true giant among mere men
Finally retiring her hard-earned title as your favorite
    pleasure

Rising Vitality

My womb throbbing and squeezing until she bleeds
A bright, full moon hanging in the black night
You, an impressive spiritual release
Manifested into a physical emancipation

Your grip weakens by the minute on these walls
A bull no longer able to dig his heels into flesh
My body purging lethal energy from inside of me
Dead dreams drip and fall away until she's anew

Pseudo Asphyxiation

Slow breath in and out, coolness touching my throat
Circling between the ebb and flow, heart beating about

Visions of my hands around your neck, amplified pleasure
Cricoid pressure as pseudo asphyxiation reflects

A premonition of your heart break twice in a moon phase
I ring no bells of warning; I watch you find your fate

Seven

Intuitives gift me the messages from beyond
Assisting my feet through residual energies
Pushing my chin up, eyes forward and ready
Trying to run before I'm ready to crawl

Simmering in the discomfort of now
Processing emotion without dwelling
The balance act in an age of lessons
One step forward, two steps back

Tapping away into emotional freedom
Singing bowls vibrate, breaking frequencies
A black string wrapping each index finger
Tension snaps the names away from each other

I still pray to my gods for your well being
I pray to my gods for protection from you
She counted seven guardian angels around me
Seven shields to hold and guard my essence

Lineage

Mother Gaia I hear your bellows and cries
I feel your pain erupt from the core to surface
I feel your heavy heart in the dreary skies
Mother Gaia, help me to lift your head up

The sisterhood of the rose beckons my name
The dormant Priestess in me rubs her eyes
Awake into the world and her beauty
Devoted delightfully sweet, slightly tart

Mother earth, soften my edges just so
Help me to embody the grid of love
Help me to step into my destined power
Show me how to seed consciousness

Unbound

Old soul stories bubble to the surface
Begging for air and acknowledgment
Ancient vows all have expiry dates
It is time to let go in love

Name them so you shall claim them
It's time to align with destiny
I carry the lessons and growth
From this day forward, I am unbound

Young Girl

I am not the same young girl you fell in love with
all those years ago

A girl who wished to never be left abandoned,
scared to be alone

A girl that compromised and broke off pieces of
her to sustain you

A girl with a newborn intuition and trauma healing
long overdue

I am not the same young girl you took for granted
and cast aside

A girl who kneeled and handed her heart over that
you could deny

A girl whose loyalty was unwavering and unques-
tionable in character

A girl who obsessed over your needs without hers
ever being a factor

I am not the same young girl that would turn the
other cheek and look away

A girl whose heart bled on the floor after
devastating and callous filets

A girl who mopped her own blood with blurry eyes
and an empty chest cavity

A girl that took the leap of faith you asked of her
despite feeling gravity

I am not the same young girl that cried herself to
   sleep while you slept soundly

A girl whose sorrow turned to exhaustion,
   eventually turning to rage profoundly

A girl who held tight to the single rope of someday
   dreams you threw her once

A girl who kept your dark, dirty secrets as rocks
   on her chest weighing a ton

I am not the same young girl that looked at
   you with stars inside her eyes

A girl whose gaze saw what you were capable
   of and dismissed it as all lies

A girl that saw the potential of who you could be
   if you just tried harder

A girl who had no realization of who she was
   or her birthright of power

I am not the same young girl you fell in love with
   all those years ago

A girl who blindly took your hand, allowing
   you to lead while she followed

A girl who chose to grow up and become a young woman
   with grit and verve

A woman who cloaks herself in self-love and knows
   exactly what she deserves

Nerite Snails

No distractions this time. No new lovers. No new messages.
Just me, myself, and I. Just old silence. Just new lessons.

Letting my skin crawl as I feel my feels without a vice
Letting the discomfort envelop my being should suffice

Maybe it's atonement. Maybe it's healing. Maybe it is
    what it is.
Dreams of being a Mrs. on hold until I'm comfortable
    being a miss

Logic pulling me to the right, emotions harshly to the left
I feel my insides pull apart into two starting inside my
    chest

Tears surface during sunny walks without any warning sign
Not sure if I'm really losing my shit or if I'm fine

I picture the pain as nerite snails digesting debris inside
    of me
Keeping an ecosystem functioning during repair until it's
    free

I roll my eyes remembering when I said I wanted to feel
    everything
Well here I am sitting in my manifestation, blinded by
    the swing

Uncharted territory carries with her fear, change, and no
    direction
Closed eyes and crossed fingers, I jump and pray for my
    resurrection

The Lies I Tell Myself

Sitting in the junkyard of the lies you tell and the
    promises you break,
I tell myself I can clean it up all alone and everything
    will be okay

You're the needle in my arm, ready to push, not sure if
    I should
I tell myself I won't overdose again right before I lose
    my airway

I ride you back and forth until my eyes roll rear and
    euphoria discharges
I tell myself I won't get attached despite multiple
    oxytocin releases

I simultaneously dream of a future and watch your every
    move and word
I tell myself I'm in control this time until I find
    myself in pieces

Revoked Access

My heart used to jump into my throat when I saw your
    number on my phone
Now, my heart doesn't move, and my throat doesn't open
    to speak

I wish you well and I wish you safe but, what is there
    left to say?
What's done is done, you'll only find harsh
    silences if you seek

Forgive

As I learn to forgive myself
I can forgive you too

Marrow

As I fall in love with myself
I learn to set healthy boundaries

Learning to pause before responding
Learning how to keep my cup full

Accepting my light and darkness
As equal parts that make me, me

Filling my marrow with my kindness
I start to blossom into my best self

Learning how to choose me first
Holding space for my soul to heal

Giving myself my everything and all
The way I tried to give myself to you

Self-Acceptance

I black out the canvas of love
Until it looks unfamiliar to me
I rip my eyes out of my skull
Feeling my way through the dark

My feet slowly scuffle forward
My hands outreached and motioning
Until it becomes choreography
Dancing my way through the dark

Mirror reflections nonexistent
My heart beat echoes in my ears
Until it becomes a hymn
Singing my way through the dark

Alone in my conversations
Keeping company with myself
Unfamiliarity becoming normal
Loving myself through the dark

I Miss Me

I miss the way I laugh and breathe
When I know who I am
I miss my perception of my
Reflection when I know what I am

I miss my altruistic nature
The essence of my being
I miss the way I hold myself
In such a high regard

I miss how I think being smart
Is more important than being pretty
I miss how I bask in
Having a queer, unique nature

I miss how confident I am
In speaking my truth
I miss how I hold everyone
Accountable for their actions

Most of all
I miss how easy it feels
Being in my own skin
I miss me being me

Dear Me

Can you forgive me for betraying you for so many years?
Can you forgive me for becoming the very girl you despise?
Can you forgive me for losing my nerve and voice?
Can you forgive me for allowing them to bend my reflection?

Can you forgive me for being ashamed of you?
Can you forgive me for allowing footsteps on your back?
Can you forgive me for trying to blend into the crowd?
Can you forgive me for begging for anyone's acceptance?

Can you forgive me for putting your needs last?
Can you forgive me for putting love over dignity?
Can you forgive me for putting him on a pedestal?
Can you forgive me for putting you in a basement?

Can you forgive me for selling you out?
Can you forgive me for quelling your ambition?
Can you forgive me for settling for less?
Can you forgive me for trying to stay small?

Can you forgive me for reading gossip instead of books?
Can you forgive me for letting them chisel you down?
Can you forgive me for hating you so much?
Can you forgive me for almost sabotaging destiny?

Can you forgive me for losing my way?
Can you forgive me for not knowing what I was doing?
Can you forgive me for my addictions?
Can you forgive me for not staying true to myself?

Please forgive me.

Say When

Wincing when I tell my reflection I love her
Perhaps it's from feeling undeserving
After the ways in which I mistreated her

I simultaneously begin to make amends with
Her and the abusive thoughts in my head
Leaning in close, she whispers, "Say when."

Uncle.

Lilith in Sagittarius

Horse hair brush in hand and I dip new hues
Spreading tincture over primed context
Yesterday is done, I can't undo it
Looking back causing cervical strain

Neck stiff in a brace to keep eyes forward
I haven't been blessed with amnesia yet
But in the corner, I catch her dancing and
I remember and see who I was before the pain

She sways uninhibited and unapologetic
She can tell a story without one word
In awe I watch her magically exist
Laughing at them trying to keep her tamed

She spindles worth into my cracks and breaks
Patiently, she waits for my bones to solidify
She reminds me in time, I'll be dancing too
In time, all soul pieces can be reclaimed

Never For Sale

I sold my soul to the devil himself
In exchange for
False safety and an impossible dream

I'm taking it back since it was
Never for sale
Or his to own in the first place

DNA

The parts of you are
In the parts of me
Encoded as warnings
Encoded as wisdom

Great grandmothers are
Swimming in my veins
Allowing me to become
Their answered pleas

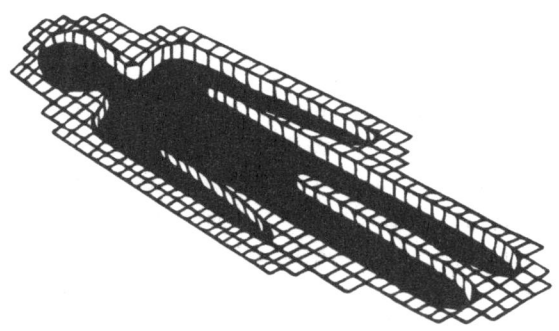

An Answered Prayer

She speaks to God on a tear stained pillow
As she lies next to a sleeping husband
Filled with belated self-awareness
She asks Him to let me be what she was not

Hitched her wagon onto someone else's star
Without knowing who she truly was
Thinking marriage would equate fulfillment
Confident she had the recipe for happiness

The love she was starved from as a child
A longing to be completed, taken care of
Did not come after the wedding cake was cut
It did not come when she made them fathers

Her aimless wagon was dragged and buried
By the time she knew who she truly was
Marriage had equated to codependency
When she looked closely at the ingredients

Her daughter managed to evolve and be better
While still managing to follow in her footsteps
Each generation finding their own damned cycle
Without a role model for self-worth and value

She prays I can break free to build a new template
Drawing on my inner strength needed to do so
She prays for me to find and know my own creed
To live a life more joyful than I could ever imagine

Patience

Someday will come when I'm good and ready
Someday I will be someone's faithful wife
Someday I will be someone's devoted mother
Someday is not today, and that's more than okay

Standards

We don't drink poison
Because we are thirsty

I Will Pray For You

You will search for my eyes in every girl you meet for
  the rest of your life
You will try to fill the void you feel in your soul from
  losing my heart
You will lose countless hours of sleep, haunted at 3 am
  by the ghost of me
You will pray and dream for a miracle for me
  to return for years to come

You will tell everyone that you wish me well, but it was
  honestly for the best
You will tell some that I'm a monster and curse the day I
  was born
You will pretend you're moving on and live it up like a
  bachelor should
You will find someone new, love her even, but she'll nev-
  er hit the same

You will cry the day you hear I am finally
  married, knowing all hope is dead
You will see my children and your heart will ache, wish-
  ing they were yours
You will hear my voice again someday, your heart dropping
  into your stomach
You will run into me by accident in ten years, full of
  fluttering butterflies

I will ask God to help you to stop searching
  for me in any other woman
I will ask God that He heal your heart and
  allow you to forget me in time
I will ask God that He banish your ghosts,
  allowing you to sleep through the night
I will ask God to help you to find new miracles to pray and
  dream for yourself

I will hope you tell everyone all of the things I
    taught you about love
I will hope you tell some that I was a great gift
    and lesson to learn
I will hope you find peace and learn to slow down
    and find what truly matters
I will hope you love someone new and she is
    better for you than I was

I will pray for you to find self-forgiveness from
    your self-sabotage
I will pray for you to find the strength to
    be genuinely happy for me someday
I will pray for you to find yourself and learn
    from all of your mistakes
I will pray for you, knowing you have to live with
    regret for the rest of your life

Emerge

Holding my heart like an egg
Incubating her into warmth
Waiting while she grows
Until she is ready to emerge

This

Of course, it still hurts deeply, sweet girl
You gave it everything you possibly had
You thought it was happily ever after but
Your tower of dreams came crashing down

Of course, you're still disappointed
There was potent potential you could taste but
You put your eggs into someone else's basket
The boy was disastrously careless and clumsy

Yes, you're covered in soot from head to toe
From everything turning into rubble and dust but
Look up, over there to the horizon sweet girl
Destiny and fate have yet to kiss you with blessings

Yes, you're scared to walk on a path, mapless
Scared of making a mistake or missing opportunity
Only look back to see how far you have come
You will look back and see how much you have grown

This is where you carve your own path, sweet girl
This is where the magic happens and unfolds
This is where the universe tickles you with surprises
This is where your wildest dreams can finally come true

Prince Consciousness

Instead of asking how much of your time is left:
Ask him how much of your mind, baby

The Alchemist (Paulo Coelho)

..."What is a warrior of the light?"
"You already know that," she replied with a smile
"She is someone capable of understanding the miracle of life,
Of fighting to the last for something she believes in-
And of hearing the bells that the waves set ringing on the seabed."

She never thought of herself as a Warrior of the Light.
The woman seemed to read her thoughts.
"Everyone is capable of these things.
And, though no one thinks of herself as a Warrior of Light,
We all are."

She looked at the blank pages in the notebook.
The woman smiled again.
"Write about the warrior," she said.

Sweetener

Gliding my poise through dreams
A sweetener, like
Sunday morning pancakes through syrup

No Regrets

As long as I live life
With no regrets
With love
With giving
With joy
I will always be able
To live with myself

Always

I appreciate the universe
For what it is
On my terms

I always have,
And I always will

Still

And for those that still
Persecute and slander
Misunderstand and demean
I pray for you too

Home

What was once a hazard in the mirror
Is now an asset, an ally

Now, I call my name
And she feels like home

Liberated

Her mouth opens to inhale
Her diaphragm pushing
She holds it, for a second
Keeping her eyes closed

Her green iris' flash open
Her lungs release into the air
The corner of her lip curls
Liberated, healthy, secure, blissful

Prophetic Dreams

Your mouth spills a version of the truth
The stain marks me for life

Upon the surface, you're collected
Underneath, a beast screams to be unleashed

Your mouth spills another lie
Of which only I am privy to catch

You tell on yourself in my dreams
I collect my data quietly, unknowingly

Clarity brings anger before peace
I silently whisper goodbye

Mirage

Closed fists clutching to her truth
They whisper but no one speaks up
Watching a thorn crown placement
They witness but don't look away

The vagabond knows her decree
Searing 40 days and nights
Scorched sun and a glass of wine
Secrets unearthed as she slept

She wanders further to the outskirts
Until her silhouette waves with the heat
Until she becomes a figment of your
Imagination upon the horizon

Buried.

Earth bitten underneath fingernails
Raw hands under running water
Old stagnant energy lingers
They point and yell Witch.
Cause she bloomed

Air Tight

Ask the lightning bug
What happens when
You let them
Jar your light

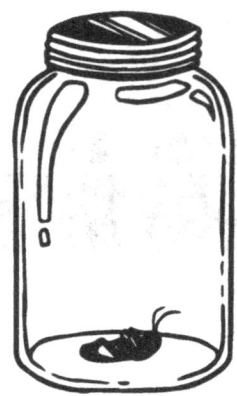

Chasing Freedom

Gunning down 91 with the windows down
Singing at the top of my lungs

Purgatory

Who shall hold you tight each night
Whispering comfort in your ear
When you wake up in a cold sweat

Inebriated by the vividness yet
Startled by the sudden reality
As I haunt you in your dreams?

Pain for Everyone

We scream love is love, let them live
Yet they too are fallible to heartache

Tap Your Heels

Someday I'll wish upon a star
And wake up where the shrouds
Are far behind me
Where I'm finally sick of your shit
And I can see this for all that it is
Where you can never find me

Somewhere over the rainbow
Bluebirds fly
Birds don't cry over the rainbow
Why then, oh why, can't I?

If happy little birds defy
Beyond the rainbow
Why, oh why can't I?

Breaking the Cycle

It is a tango we step into
Each generation learning
The choreography from
Their mothers and fathers

Fathers leading our mothers
Into darkness and despair
One and two and three and four
We find our familiar dance partners

Perpetuating the cursed dance
The broken record never stops
I find my father in dance halls
Until the trauma blows out my eardrums

So I became tone deaf to the
Same old song and dance
Within I feel my own rhythm
Birthing a new pirouette

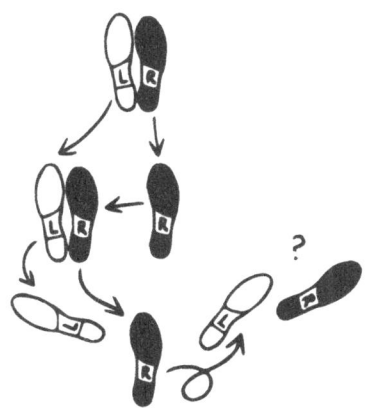

Outnumbered

I can find it within my heart to forgive you
Let it all go for the sake of peace
But the way my ancestors are set up...

Wild women who were detained and imprisoned
As submissive wives and unwilling mistresses
Raped. Molested. Sold. Beaten. Abandoned. Abused.

Softness bruised and torn apart by men
Men led by their ego, power and pride
You, the last man of that kind in this line

And for that, my friend, you have unleashed
A thousand years of a thousand women's
Burning rage and suppressed spirits

You should have known better than to think
I come from a line of meek and mild females
Simply because they lived in cages

Fool. You called yourself a zookeeper.
The lioness called out to her pride for help
And you, well now, you're simply outnumbered.

Sleep tight.

One More

Heavy heart, still beating
Healing heart, still bleeding
Blindfolded in the dark
Leading herself by sound

The dreamer became afraid to dream
Each abandonment taking a bit of hope
The colored scenes in her head
Feeling like foolish wishes now

She boxes excitement to leave it alone
She couldn't possibly feel it again
Hope always brought her pain and
Back to the cemetery of unfulfilled dreams

Each burial and mourning harder than the next
Taking a piece of her heart down as she
Lays them 6 feet down below the earth
Eventually learning to numb it out

The dust whispers, "What about one more?"
Shaking her head, she says absolutely not
Laughing, the wind picks up and reveals
A golden string attached to her heart

Bewildered, confused, and scared because
She feels excitement flutter in her chest
Again since the last funeral. The dust says
To follow her heart. "One more."

Release

My great great great grandmothers'
DNA burrowed into my marrow
Inactivated capsule seedling
Nurtured by my blood

Sprouting dense roots, she
Begins to stretch her arms
Bones and hips crack as
She awakens in my veins

Travelling and assessing
Each cell inside of me
Her medicine to my pain
She clutches my hurt

And she crawls up my spine
Spouting out of the lotus
On top of my crown as
We release each other

The Army

"How did the men conquer us?"

"They separated us."

1000

Don't you know young girl?
You aren't just here
To liberate yourself

Spread your wings to fly
And you shall liberate
The 1000 women before you

Blood

Your Spanish conquistador blood
Was out to make me a conquest
Drunk off of usurped power
As all the masculines before

Unfortunate timing now since
The veil is thinning out and
I remember my own Viking blood
As I am simply unconquerable.

Guided

Gathering in the dense wood
They whisper in my ear
Guided, fiercely protected

Try and separate us now

Wounded Masculine

Their masks slip as they fall under her trance
Drunk off of her unassuming dynamism
Following her as far as she lets them
Ready to lose it all for another stroke

In the morning the hangover hits and
They find themselves naked and alone
Their infected wound sutures dehisced
With a mirror facing every shadow

Show me

Show me a self-healed man and I
Shall show my soft femininity

Peace Treaty

My eyes flutter closed as I
Bathe in vivid consciousness

I've been waiting for my moment
Of justice, she's consistently late

My wicked wounds remain open
And have left me desiring revenge

Girl, you can't take karma into your
Own hands without getting them dirty

I pray for myself every night.
I pray you learn to leave me alone.

She tells me I should start praying
For you to have a good life too

She tells me she sees how heavy the
Burden is, and I can put it down any time

But this globe on my back feels as if it's
Melted into my skin. It's mine.

Put it down, Lay it down. Let it all go.
But that feels like surrendering the war.

Exactly. She says.

Momma's Smile

Momma's smile changes an entire day,
Melted gold in the cracks of flaws

Too bad I haven't heard her belly laugh
Since before we laid her first love to rest

Intellectually intertwined, complex, confusing
She's been locked in the basement of her mind

Confined, wounded, with the saddest green eyes
Heavy heart barely beating most days

I just want to see you soar so you can smile
Giving everything out until there's nothing left

Your life stunted and stagnant before it began
I just want to see you smile again, momma.

She reaches her arms out of her cage to
Touch my face and say, "it's okay baby."

Who wants to see their mother corralled?
Who wants to listen to her cry to sleep?

I've tried picking and hammering the locks
Nothing works and I can't leave her here alone

She reaches her arms out of her cage to
Hug me and says, "It's okay for you to go."

Releasing me from my guilt because she knows
I've always wanted to spread my wings and fly

She just wants to see me soar so I can smile
Maybe in saving myself, I save her too.

Little Pond

The altitude and sunshine beckons me
Across this impeditive continent
I'm not running anymore, I swear
I'm just finally chasing my dreams

Where they can't slow me down or
Attempt to tame my nature so I
Fit into their ideal archetype
Where I'm too far away to be hurt

I still dream of green summers
And there's no fall foliage quite
Like the ones in New England
My roots are enmeshed into my being

Plants only grow as big as their containers
Tired of being a big fish in a little pond
Tired of pretending to be small and content
When I want to grow wild and free elsewhere

Wash Day

The sky claps and drums as it opens
Lightening illuminating the tops of trees
Barefoot she steps into the chaos
Until she starts dancing with the elements

A smile as wide as when she was seven
Twirling and jumping up and down
Until her hair is soaked through
Slapping her shoulders and upper back

Eyes closed, her face kissing the sky
She pretends she's a tree and sways
With her fingertips stretched out
Letting it wash all of her aching away

Peanut Pond

I heard my answers at the open space
My dry throat swallowing hard
Synchronicities dusting everything
Do you trust fate, little girl?

Patriarchy

I just want to feel as free as a child
Until the last moments of my life

Grow up girl. Get a job. Have a baby.
Where's the fun in monotony?

Why should my child be my only solace
For a life of pain? What example is that?

Living my life so I never get captured
Brought back to the farm and sheared down

Peaking around corners before dashing the hall
While the devil sleeps next to the prototype

They'll find the gasoline trails soon in
The morning. Burn the motherfucker down.

Grace

Maybe if I keep wandering and dancing
Off of the side of the crowd
I'll get lost
And eventually, find myself

Love Notes to Myself

We don't have to be what they want
We don't have to be what they desire
You can be anything you want
You can be anyone you want

We don't have to highlight our hair
We don't have to mind our manners
They never have to anyways
No one expects anything of them anyways

You measure your waist and inspect every
Inch of your body because no one
Has ever told you to inspect your
Humanity. Girl, you're more.

You're more than the play thing
That lies on her back for 30 seconds
You're more than the trophy on
His arm for the faces to impress

You're more than the plan he expects
Your mind is more beautiful than he knows
Your dreams are more vivid than his eyes
Could ever comprehend

Don't be discouraged. You're worthy of love
Not the cheap type he wrapped in tinfoil
And called it gold on Christmas morning
You deserve more than hollow words and facades

Maybe Daddy left you when you were three
What right does that give him to throw it
In your face and say you have 'daddy issues?'
What kind of monster weaponizes your wounds?

Don't get discouraged. You're worthy of peace
Not the temporary type of silence he imposed
After you tried to hold him accountable again
You deserve more than being left unheard

I know sometimes you think men are horrible
But the wicked ones are just boys who
Never knew how to really grow up
Keep the faith, good men exist mama

We don't have to play by the rules
We can dance out of step
We can paint out of the lines
We can do anything and everything

You don't have to hate yourself
To shimmy into a mold that will
Suffocate and kill you anyways
Why don't you love yourself instead

Why don't you do something wild, do
Something passionate and get called crazy
They're going to judge you anyways
Why don't you just bloom that nature

Bloom until your leaves infect the garden
Killing the vines wrapped around our necks
Like nooses and snakes
Bloom until you're free

Soul Retrieval

Pieces of her soul scattered
Held in safe keeping
Until she was ready
To call them back home

Fluttering back into her
Snowflakes drifting into
Their former places and
Seamlessly fitting in

Wisdom

Peace is only the halfway point to healing.
Standing in your power is the sign of healing

Mirror Mirror on the Wall

You rage rage rage and rage against the machine little girl
Blaming and casting your horror on the men around you

Foam dripping off of your sharp tongue as well-deserved karma
Slicing into their flesh until you wince in agony

Looking down, you have cut your own dermis and as you look
Up, all you see are mirrors surrounding you

You see this child blaming and casting horror
At the reflection staring back at her

Perhaps you choose lovers that half-love and abandon you
Because you half-love and abandon yourself

Perhaps you despise men who are controlling and rageful
Because you control and rage yourself all the time

Perhaps you judge and condemn others
Because you judge and condemn yourself

Your darkest shadows mirrored back
Beckoning to be acknowledged and loved

Tell me girl, who truly is the enemy?

Gold Dust Woman

Goddess of chaos comes to rise
Searing fire from her lover's tongue
Singeing the hair left on his ego
Her throat loosens to well ancient shrieks

A devil's mark accusation, a cheap claim
She dances and sings forward nonetheless
A wave of destruction left in her path
Or did she just pull your shadow to light?

Let Go In Peace

Past tense lover I can let go in peace
I see the skeletons and I have let them dance
I have let them humble me into pockets of grief
I have grown out of holes with clearer eyes

We were divinely connected and interwoven
To teach and love each other lessons
We are, too, divinely guided to part
To teach and love each other lessons

I have begun to find me, again
Did you write down your notes?
This next part will hurt, I'm sure
But I promise it's for the greater good

I'm so much more than how you left me.
You probably wouldn't recognize me now
There is a new path beckoning a dance
This time, I'm never coming back.

Tub

You had no idea what you were doing
You just knew there was more for you
Submerged yourself into scalding water
To cleanse your conditioning
To begin your lifelong unlearning

You broke your own heart and
Confined yourself to solitude
Your arms cold and empty
For many days and nights
Months your heart didn't sing

I used to look back and think
What a foolish naïve girl
I felt shame and disappointment
Pompous pride that I was now "better"
With an ungrateful attitude

Without her courage to step into the dark
Without her unwavering blind faith
That things will eventually turn around
Without her seed of self-love and respect
Despair would be the only color I knew

She is me and I am her
Where she stops and I begin is seamless
But I cannot be me without her
Blind courage girl, thank you
Thank you. Thank you.

Freedom

Oil changed; every bag packed
Full tank, 4 am here she goes

She's finally ready to leave
It all behind in the East

Her eyes well blurry as she
Crosses the I-70 threshold

Spreading her wings, she can
Finally taste true freedom

Open roads full of potential
Because she's got herself

Shell Shocked

An environment calm, quiet
A nervous system, enraged
Fighting in her sleep

The war ended the day she left
A battleground full of ghosts
Haunting the eerie stillness

Self-Soothing or My Undoing

Distractions
Red wine
Bubble baths
Tear stained cheeks

Resurrections
I'm fine
Feelings over facts
Bear reigned needs

Husk

If I don't belong here?
If I don't belong there?
Are dreams of restitute
Damned to be involute?

Promises to My Son

She tells me to close my eyes
As I reach into the velvet bag alone
One by one I pick out the stones
"Throw them," she says

She tells me there's a boy
A spirit who needs me to be
A different woman so he
Can fulfill his purpose when he comes

Do you want to be normal?
If you don't use them, you'll lose them
She carefully reminds me then
Or do you want to be yourself?

Baby, Momma's learning and budding
Be patient with me as I grow anew
I promise, when I'm ready for you
I'll be all you need and more

Circles

She reminds me, people can only meet you
As deeply as they've met themselves
I've met myself in each circle of hell
Nine layers of pain like a carousel

A carnival of horrors and decimation
Death wrung out over brimstone
Trying to catch a breath in a
Cloud of thick smoke

The more time I spend here,
The more I understand Morning star
If everybody else is doing it,
The less shame and guilt we have to bear

Please tell me my sweet love,
How many rings have you survived?
How many burns and scars can you count?
How many battles have you derived?

Lock and Key

Falling for you was like drinking water
For the first time after a drought
It was like coming home to a house
That had my favorite creature comforts

Falling for you was effortless, immediate
The way your lips touched mine first
In the second wooden booth
Of our bar on Larimer Street

I could see the rest of my life
When I laid my head on your chest
And you played with my hair
Kissing my forehead in between

The way you held me and spoke to me
When I told you what happened to me
The way you didn't care at all
About my heavy past and trauma

How peaceful it felt playing music
While we prepped and cooked together
How you didn't tease me when I
Ruthlessly burned the oil and rosemary

The way you refused to raise your voice
When I got triggered and defensive
The way you refused to engage
When I tried to get under your skin

I'll never forget the moment you said
"I don't see anyone else but you.
Everyone else around me is fuzzy."
When you said, "You know when you know."

How I screamed "I love you I love you I love you"
In my head for weeks on end
Wine courage allowed the words to spill
As a quiet secret in the night

It replays in my head over and over
The moment you admitted effortless
That you've been madly in love
With me since the second date

When did your pride get the best of you?
When did you let the fear run wild?
You've never been this close
You've never been this challenged

You've gotten by undetected
But I can see you to the core
You can't hide your wounds with me
You can't ignore your shadow with me

Self-preservation emotes and protects
You pretend you don't know how to swim
With me into the depths of intimacy
You begin to wear the false mask

I can't force you to find courage
I can't reassure you that you're safe
I can't make you love yourself
I can't do all the work myself

My heart begins to weep when I
Realize the limitations you impose
A chest filled with wild grief and anger
How could you do this to us?

We both have a scar on our upper lip
I was the one who understood Copper's name
The connection we discovered over Islay
Endless synchronicities, unbecoming

How could you be home but lock me out?

Shallow.

I realized I was drowning myself
In shallow pools of another's mind
In a desperate attempt to find depth

I loosen the notches in my belt
Like dead weight falling to the floor
And dive headfirst into my own breadth

Grown.

Calm. Cool. Collected.
Intuition confirmed.
I've been here before
Different man, same lie

This time, I'm grown.
I wake him from a slumber
Gently, I whisper in his ear:
"Get the fuck out of my house."

Everything.

My intuition screams
Like a hawk in the night
My intuition alarms
Like a third eye camera

When I really listen
Take her heed, caution
She tells me everything
I need to know.

The Living Ghost

Just like the others before you
You'll think you can shake me
In a few months' time
You stupid fucking fool

My memory is a slow burn
That will hurt more and more
With each passing day
As I haunt your subconscious

You'll catch my scent in public
And the room will begin to cave
As your stomach turns violently
Color draining from your face

Sleep will evade you as you as
My laughter fills your head
Regret gnaws and bruises your ego
As you lie still in the dark

Fear will grip your heart
As your messages go unanswered
Your calls never go through
As I become the living ghost.

Pause

Deep breath girl.
Deep breath.
You got this.

Him.

Dating a spiritual woman is a test
Potential initiation for
Spiritual growth, evolution

If they can't rise up to meet you
Send them on their way back to God
To face Him and explain themselves.

Growth.

Hurt instincts.
Vindictive thoughts.
Pause.
Remember.
We've come too far
To be pulled back

Done.

Sometimes the most loving thing
You can do for someone
Is to allow them to feel the
Full consequences of their actions

Capabilities

I know I'm perfectly capable
Of stooping lower to filet you
The difference between us?
I'm choosing peace instead

I Trust You

I trust you Universe
My ears are open
My eyes are clear

I know you didn't
Bring me this far
To only come this far

Messages from the Universe

Did you finally learn your lesson?

Are you ready for the next level?

Are you finally who you say you are?

Are you ready to step into your power?

Are you ready to step into your purpose?

Are you ready to be the love of your life?

It's Easy

It's easy to blame the drug addict father
For all of her romantic mishaps and failures
But why does no one talk about the mother
Who invalidates, manipulates, breadcrumbs
    and gaslights?

Responsible.

Your feelings, your needs, your thoughts
Trumped mine
My truth, my cries, my pleads
Unnoticed

The child that spoke the truth
Shamed
The girl who wanted freedom
Chained

You had to keep me close
Needed me
Yet you resented all my
Individuality

Because I went with the flow
You thought
You could mold me like clay
At will

Your time. Your terms. Your taste.
Never to be questioned
My silence. My severity. My survival.
A quiet, devastating tsunami

Years in the making, you could say
My voice. My confidence. My boundaries.
My grace. My dreams. My song.
You're not my responsibility.

Right.

My boldness disrupts self-deception
So, I must be the problem, right?

Blue Heat

Reclaiming the velvet between my thighs
Who am I to become?
Smoke billowing between flames
Fog kissing mountain dew
She topples over in blue heat
Pooled wax lying still, noble
She is the vessel which
Merges two universes
From the ash, she will rise

I have nothing to be ashamed of

Compulsion

I spit the blood that has pooled in my mouth
Out onto the cool, damp concrete
Knees kissing the floor, my fingers supporting
The weight of the entire world

I close my eyes in an attempt
To find a moment of contentment
Peace elusive and cunning
My will spilling out of my eyes

Knock after knock, blow after blow
Am I getting stronger or more cynical?
Perhaps this is as far as I go
Destined for misery and heartache it seems

My thoughts merging together like a category 5
Looking for directions on a deserted highway
In the middle of nowhere, starved of hope
Perhaps this is where they all win, I lose

Nauseous, legs and spirit too weak to stand
Compulsively, I decide to crawl
Gravel piercing my knees and palms
I think to myself, this is just masochistic

"Nah." A voice inside booms
"You don't get to give up."

Conversations with Pain

Sit with me child, she whispers to me tenderly
She juts her finger inside my open, gaping wound
A breathlessness cry erupts from my throat
I double over and curl into myself

What do you feel child? She asks me
Nauseated, I hold my stomach and dry heave
My neck dripping beads of hot sweat
My skin an inferno ready to erupt

She pushes her finger deeper into my wound
My consciousness begins to go in and out
Visions of childhood memories flood
Tears erupt down my dirty, tired cheeks

She sticks her finger in until she can
Touch the back of my spine
She grabs hold of the grief, the confusion
The hurts, the sorrows and gently pulls them out

Like a baby through a slit in my abdomen
She places them on my chest
Here. She says. Sit with them child.
Heed the lessons that they can teach you.

Salve

Baby's first heartache without a vice
Wobbling like a toddler finding balance
Emotions knocking me to the floor
Language too underdeveloped for instincts

I can feel every crevice and crack
The holes you impaled upon me
The holes impaled by others that
I pretended no longer existed

It hurts. It hurts. It hurts.
But I don't try to salve the wound
I let her bleed out freely
Becoming fertilizer in the midst of rawness

Machismo

It's a dry, dark morning here
In the wild, wild west

Grace allotting a moment of
Silence in a head full of chatter

I can see from here that
It's cold in your house

You're crying when no one
Is watching

Blaming yourself for being
Selfish and cunning

Flying to the east next
To the moon in the sky

How powerful do you feel knowing,
The machismo has bested you

Necromancy

Can I stop building my own coffins?
Can I stop being a haunted memory?
Would it be necromancy to resurrect
Alive and well after an emotional murder?

Lady-Like

What does it mean to be lady-like?
Does it mean contorting your spine
Into a fold as the vessel sucks you in
Your breathing restricted, every move
Every word chosen carefully to be digestible
Applause and smiles for being a good girl
Pretending and minimizing the misogyny
Fawning for attention, a need to be chosen
A painted mask always smiling, never fusses
Is undoubtably a sweet and slow suicide

     Fuck that.　Choke on all of me
       motherfuckers.

Emotional Freedom

Conditions placed on a little girl
Only loved when seen and not heard
A girl grows into a lifelong
Occupation of dissecting and shelving

The least digestible aspects of herself
Becoming palatable to a man' gaze
Who could never love all parts of her
Only the parts that serve his ego

Put the scalpel down, girl.
Be a goddamn beautiful mess.
Be emotional. Angry. Ugly. Loud.
Be feral. Instinctive. Proud. Confident.

Take your first breath of a new life
Drink and fill from your own fountain
Your emotional freedom lies in
Unconditional self-love

Jolene's Reply

Me oh my, dear Dolly, sorry to hear that
He's been calling out my name absentmindedly
In his sleep, while you lie awake in agony

For what it's worth, dear Dolly
Only perhaps in another life
Would I ever want to be his wife

But dear Dolly, I promise you
He's only a small chapter in my book now
I'm on a new page far from your vows

Sometimes I wonder, dear Dolly, about you
Memorizing my flesh and laughter and design
Comparing your exceptional features to mine

Why are you scared of losing your man?
Does he walk right through you as he comes home
Dear Dolly, as you feel unseen and wholly unknown

Why do you kneel on rice and wait, dear Dolly
For this man to notice your martyrdom, to choose you
Despite your knees all scarred and bruised

Dear Dolly, help me to understand how you
Worship a man as your one and only sweetheart
Whom has a harem of secret admirers' in safeguard

I know what it's like, dear Dolly
To love a man so deeply it hurts
Worse than self-betrayal can subvert

Should the voice of reason in your head
Dear Dolly, remind you that you deserve more
I've attached a bus pass that you didn't ask for

It's never too late to change your mind, dear Dolly
No matter how much you find yourself devoted
To a saccharine lie that's simply sugar-coated

Legendary.

Only some of my exes
Are from Texas

But every single one of 'em
Will breathlessly admit

That the way I loved 'em
Is something they can't forget

That I was, that I still am
Forever remembered as the goddamn

Greatest cowgirl
In the entire world

Last Sunday Drive

We climbed another path in the Rocky Mountains
In an ode to the adventures we shared
As we explored this new state
Together over the last year

Two east coast girls fated to be friends
Around an unfamiliar Aspen tree
You made a strange place feel like home
And I can't thank you sufficiently

Looking back, I can see clearly how the
Memories we made will be some
Of my most cherished, prized possessions
I could have only ever dared to dream of

I was midflight of shedding my old skin
As I began to feel my new
I didn't have to be anything other
Then who I chose to show up and debut

The mountains soothed my trauma
I released and relinquished my pain
You always showed up with a smile
In complete acceptance of me again

No matter what season I was weathering
Through my heartbreak and confusion
You were my trusted sounding board
As I was learning to ground profusion

My lips curl in a bittersweet motion
As I listen to you giggle and say
You don't understand this song
And you hate 2 PMs on Sundays

We promise each other this isn't the end
We'll be friends forever, we're bonded
But acknowledge this shared, sacred chapter
Is closing now as we begin to look beyond

You laugh and smile kindly as the tears
Unabashedly fall down my cheeks
And I begin to laugh too because
I simply can't stop the leak

We throw each other off of our shoulders
Admonishing the security blanket we've known
You glance and hug me with your eyes
Perceptive I can take the next steps alone

As I pull out of your parking spot, I begin
To play your 90's playlist, dear friend
Cause we know every new beginning comes
From some other beginning's end

Vulnerability

Finding the strength in vulnerability
Allowing my softness to be my intensity
A well-earned dose of peace and tranquility
I'm much more powerful in my intimacy

Braille

You simply cannot defeat the one
Whom has cleansed and nursed
Her own dehisced wounds for none
Other than herself, patiently, deliberately
Touching her scars as though they're simply
Now braille recounting a story intimately

1000 Layer Folded Katana

They call her Katana now
But Tamahagne before
She was folded into 1000 layers
Relentlessly rid of steel bloom

She used to smell of soft pine and charcoal
Right before she was placed in the tatara
Melded into an unrecognizable form
Referred to her as satetsu

Edges hammered ceaselessly, fold after fold
Her impurities removed, strength refined
Alternating hardness with ductility
Enhancing her toughness, lethality

They have no clothes in your presence
Peering into their soul like glass
You see clearly what tries to be hidden
One glance and they become transparent

Created to be the walking sword
Meant for breakthrough and clarity
A weapon forged to break illusion
Greatly feared, respected, venerated

206 Bones

Time is running out for you
She breathlessly tells me
Hurry, take only what you need
Don't stop, don't look back

She tells me of dunes, desolate land
Don't stop until you collapse
Completely into 206 bones
Fear captivity over death

She whispers "La Loba will find you."
Explains no further and shoves me
Forward into the blackest night
Falling stars dancing above my head

I hear the search party screaming
The hounds howling in the distance
My legs tired, yet my pace quickens
Cyanide gripped in case I don't make it

The longest night drones on and
My bare feet finally meet the sand
I don't dare think of rest
Until they have long lost my scent

When the day breaks above
The sand pelts my exposed skin
The sun pounds and burns my hide
Yet one foot follows the other

My breath and mouth become dry
The last of the water flits
On my swollen tongue
My shoulders stagger and sway

Each step into the unknown
Exposes my flesh
Until my muscle bleeds
My guts spill outside

I fall to my knees
A single tear plummets
As I close my eyes and fall
Down into the deepest sleep

I do not get up, I do not breath
The desert swallows me whole
Until all 206 of my bones
Lie scattered, hidden among the dunes

Women Who Run With the Wolves
(Clarissa Pinkola Estes)

She is called many things
To many different tongues
She searches day and night for what is lost
She collects the wolf bones, La Loba

She hand picks them up one by one
They clink as the ivory lands
Into her hand-woven basket
As she walks back to her canyon

She starts a fire on a black night
Falling stars dancing above her head
She places the bones together
On top of the red clay dirt

She begins to chant and dance
Arms swaying, reaching for the stars
The rib and leg bones begin to
Flesh out, the beast assembling fur

She sings so deeply the canyon floor shakes
A wolf shapes and takes its first breath
La Loba's feet stomps into red clay
Jumpstarting the beat into its heart

Its yellow eyes flash open mid song
Jumps up, and runs down the canyon
The moonlight hits the animal and
Is suddenly alchemized into a woman

Naked and feral, she howls at the breaking dawn
La Loba throws her head back and laughs
Clapping her hands together as the she wolf
Completely sprints free into the horizon

Welcome home.

Old Friend

Blood drips from my mouth, laughing and wide
Standing outside the devil's lair
Screaming for him to come outside

Bewildered and confused he thought
He left me for dead in the desert
Confident his crime would never be caught

A giggling hysterical assassin
Is all he sees peering out of his window
Barking his name in ludacris fashion

I bellow, "Is that all that's to come??"
"Remember this face," I tell him
"Remember my name on your serpent tongue."

My eyes glimmer and smile as they stare into
The empty fear I put behind his black eyes
"You're going to need a better follow through."

I smirk as I take a few steps away quietly
Assured I will be the bane of his existence
I throw my head back and laugh maniacally

My laughter turns to howls and my jowls grin
As I hear my kin bawl back in the near distance
"We'll be seeing you around, old friend."

To Be Continued...

Acknowledgments and References

Women Who Run With the Wolves (Clarissa Pinkola Estes) pg. 308
references the cantadora "La Loba" in Dr. Clarissa Pinkola Estes'
book Women Who Run with the Wolves. When Alyssa was only a few
pages in January 2021, she cried hysterically because she finally
felt like she fully understood herself for the first time in her
life. She references this book as her "bible" for living and
expressing her feminity.

Esté s Clarissa Pinkola. "La Loba." *Women Who Run with the*
  Wolves: Myths and Stories of the Wild Woman Archetype,
  Ballantine Books, New York, 2003, pp. 23-24.

Prince Consciousness pg. 250 references lyrics to the Purple
One's song, "Let's Go Crazy." A former ICU RN, Alyssa was in
COVID units during the first and second waves from March to
December 2020. Due to her occupation at the time, she spent the
majority of lockdown from March to May 2020 alone with her dog.
She credits Prince's music, the movie *Purple Rain* and making
weird, shitty art as the tenets of keeping her sanity during a
very weird, uncertain time. If you don't respect Prince as an
artist, you can't sit with her.

Prince and the Revolution. "Let's Go Crazy." *Purple Rain*,
  Remastered Ed, Erotic City, 1984.

The Alchemist (Paulo Coelho) pg. 250 references an excerpt from
the book The Alchemist by Paulo Coelho. She discovered this book
in 2015 and it had a profound impact on her at the time and
taught her the importance of putting your life's purpose first.

Coelho, Paulo, et al. "Warrior of the Light Prologue." *Alchemist*,
  HarperOne, San Francisco, CA, 2014, pp. 129-129.

About the Author

Alyssa Nadolny started writing poetry when she was 10-11 years old in black and white composition books that she never shared until she was 15 years old. When she finally showed them to a creative writing teacher and was invited to perform in her school's poetry slam her secret passion was opened like Pandora's box. Psychology and spirituality have been other intense passions of hers and she graduated with a DNP in psychiatry from Fairfield University in May of 2020. Born and raised in New England until the end of her Saturn Return in December 2020, she relocated to CO with her road dog/best friend/soulmate, Ollie. In her spare time you can try to find her snow-boarding or hiking the Rockies, pulling tarot cards, connecting with spirit, playing volleyball, attending farmer's markets or telling inappropriate dark jokes to her friends when she's bored. This is her first published collection of poems.

APPENDIX :: i. Kiss of Destiny

APPENDIX :: ii. Crossing the First Threshold

APPENDIX :: iii. Tests, Allies, Enemies

APPENDIX :: iv. Return With the Elixir